THE
SEASON
NEVER
ENDS

Wins, Losses, and the Wisdom of the Court

DON SHELBY

Bascom Hill Publishing Group

212 3rd Avenue North, Suite 290

Minneapolis, MN 55401

612.455.2293

www.bascomhillbooks.com

Many of the stories in *The Season Never Ends* were originally published in Full-Court Press. They are reprinted here by arrangement with and permission of Kevin Mulder and Keith Wandrei.

ISBN: 978-1-935098-69-0

LCCN: 2011900625

Distributed by Itasca Books

Cover Design and Typeset by Jenni Wheeler

Printed in the United States of America

For Coach Myron and Nancy Dickerson

CONTENTS

AUTHOR'S NOTE

These stories are based on fact. Most of them are mine. Some of them have been told to me. Except for my name and those of my family members, all names have been changed and some identifying details have been altered.

FOREWORD BY TUBBY SMITH

One of the things I know is that time doesn't change. People, places, things change, but time is constant. And the lessons of basketball don't change. As they happen to us, we may not understand what they mean, but as we grow older, we tend to look back on these experiences of our youth with a little more insight, a little more understanding. And yet, these lessons somehow remain fresh to us. Basketball, as seen through the eyes of Don Shelby in these stories, takes me back to those experiences of the game in my own life.

You will relate to the people you read about in *The Season Never Ends*—the everyday, ordinary people who seem to appear in one form or another in all of our lives. Reading about Don's childhood friend Odie Barnett, who was a lousy basketball player but an incredible trick-shot artist, I found myself thinking about the guy in my old neighborhood who could beat me at H.O.R.S.E. with unbelievable shots. Still today, when I see him, I hear: "Tubby, remember when I beat you?"

When Don writes about reporting on the start of the Gulf War as a television journalist, he also takes us back to November 22, 1963, a date I remember with remarkable clarity. But for Don, it was also a day he learned a lesson, when his Indiana high school decided not to cancel a scheduled basketball game, because, as Don writes, the principal was an old civics teacher. "For years I taught that America's greatness is not her leaders," the principal told Don many years later, "but her people and her towns and her schools. When they shot the President, I just wanted to send a message to whoever did it that they killed a man. They didn't kill us."

Each story in this book brought to my mind times I too had lived through; I look back on my own career as a ballplayer and teacher and am reminded why I became a coach. What I consider the best part of this book is how these stories about basketball—these simple tales about the different aspects of the game—are timeless, and how they reach beyond the boundaries of sport. Don reminds us in these stories that the challenges and the triumphs of the game are paralleled by the challenges and triumphs of our lives, even if we didn't understand this at the time.

In the last chapter of this book, Don gives us ten simple lessons of the game of basketball—and the game of life. These are lessons you can use in Sunday school; in the barbershop; as a Little League coach, a day care worker, a teacher, a lawyer. These experiences go beyond basketball— beyond athletics. They are lessons about life. These are the things you should carry with you. Put them in your pocket. Put them in your heart. Write them down. Share them with the young people in your life.

You will be captivated by the simplicity of the lessons that basketball teaches, but will be reminded of how hard it can be to master these life lessons sometimes. After all, basketball is an easy game to play, but one that is hard to master. As is life.

INTRODUCTION

I'm not one of those people who memorizes statistics or charts power ratings. My office colleagues often turned to me in March to help them fill out their NCAA brackets. They never asked more than once. I am terrible at guessing winners. One year, the office pool was won by the mother of one of my friends, who picked teams based on how "cute" their mascots were. She won every game.

I pick the teams I want to win, not the ones statistics tell me have a better chance. I want these teams to win because the coach has a reputation of staying in touch with his former players, or because I saw one of the team's players help up an opposing player from the floor, or because one of their guys is leading the country in assists.

I'm an old ballplayer myself, starting point guard for Royerton High, a school in the same county as a perennial state contender. I wasn't bad. Had a nice outside shot and led the team in assists. Still hold a record for most field goals made in a final tournament in the county tourney record books. I wasn't the best guy in the conference. I wasn't even the best guy on my team.

But I was—and remain—a ballplayer, so I am also a romantic, and romantics have no place making a wager of any kind. I am a romantic because I believe that basketball, well played and well coached and, most important, well enjoyed, creates magic, a potion to which each player and coach brings an ingredient. When mixed together, under the proper conditions, something lovely and honorable happens: good, honest basketball. Will a college team be better than most because the point guard, as a nine-year-old, announced his own games as he played them in the driveway and kept shooting until he hit the game-winning shot to the roar of the imagined crowd? Will a coach have a better chance of winning a game because he visited his sixth man's sick mother in the hospital? I like to think so.

I have been a television news reporter and anchor for a very long time, and I have experienced a lot: been to a lot of places, met a lot of people, and covered a lot of notable and historic events. This is not the book most people expected me to write. Most of them thought I would write about the media, or the Middle East, or energy, or the environment, or investigative journalism. My friends and family—those who know me best—knew I would write about basketball first. They knew that because they understood that behind the facade of professional attainments and accolades, I was, and remain, the kids shooting hoops in the driveway while calling his own play-by-play for the radio audience that exists only in his mind.

And, in every game he announced, his team was trailing by one point, and time was winding down, and the ball was in his hands, and he always took the last shot (sometimes over and over again). He never grew bored by the imagined sound of the crowd erupting in cheers when he hit that jump shot at the buzzer to win the game. How many times did his imaginary teammates pick him up on their shoulders and carry him off the court? They did it every time. Whatever success I've had in my life can be traced directly back to those moments. I am a long way from my driveway back home and the rickety hoop on the side of the garage, but I still want the ball in my hands when any game, of any kind, is on the line.

I wrote these stories over the last twenty-five years, in between reporting, coaching my daughters' basketball teams, playing in Old Timers' games and Senior Leagues, and life on and off court. If you are, or ever were, a basketball player, chances are you'll see yourself in these stories. They were written for you. If you weren't a ballplayer, you might, after reading these stories, look in the mirror and see a team player staring back at you.

Don Shelby
Minneapolis
November 2010

BIG JIM AND UNCLE HARRY

Teams are like families. Families are like teams.

I was glad to see that the Minnesota State Legislature passed a new law making it illegal to kill or to threaten to kill a referee. It's about time. Good referees are hard to find, and excellent ones are an endangered species. If referees were on trading cards, I'd have a collection of them. I'd have Mindy Rudolph, Jimmy Enright, and the guy who travels with the Harlem Globetrotters. And I'd have Big Jim Carrie and Uncle Harry.

Big Jim and Uncle Harry were two of the best. They were an officiating team in my neck of the woods, and the pair handled about twenty games in which I played. In most cases, Big Jim and Uncle Harry were better entertainment than the ballplayers. To start with, Big Jim was huge. He stood 6'7" and weighed roughly a ton. Once, at the beginning of a game in which none of the players was taller than six foot, Big Jim didn't throw the ball up for the jump; he dropped it down. If Big Jim was notable for being big, Uncle Harry was equally well known for being small. Together, they looked like Laurel and Hardy in stripes.

Big Jim was also the county sheriff when the Democrats were in office. He was used to the authority he wielded, and he issued technical fouls like parking tickets. He tossed Charlie Hixon out of one game for saying "Sheesh!" Big Jim was such a show-off that when he was ready to present the ball to a foul shooter, he'd palm the ball, hold it out in front of the players, lift up two of his fingers so he was holding the ball with the remaining three, smile, and say, "Two shots, gentlemen."

Both men were expressive and theatric. They played to the crowd and their stage was the area in front of the scorer's table. When a foul was called in the lane, a whistle would sound and one of them would come charging out from under the basket toward the stage in front of the scorer's table, shouting, "No, no, no. He can't do that around here! Number two-three gets him going up..." Here he would simulate the whole foul sequence, slamming his hand into his own forearm. Then he would turn his back on the audience and walk toward the foul line, letting the tension build. Suddenly, he'd turn and say, "And the basket is good! We'll shoot one."

I should mention that 'Uncle Harry' isn't a nickname. Uncle Harry was my uncle, and the uncle of about fifteen other Shelbys who played in the conference. But all the other players and fans called him Uncle Harry, too. That started right after the first game he refereed, in which one of his nephews was playing. He had called a charging foul on a Shelby, and the kid turned around and yelled, "Aw, Uncle Harry!" From that day on, whenever he blew a call, the crowd responded in unison: "Aw, Uncle Harry!"

The most distinct memory I have of the duo comes from the very first game I saw them call. I was a freshman called up to dress for the varsity for one away game. My dad said I was there to take up space inside someone else's uniform. But that was okay. The guy whose place I took was a center, and his uniform was five sizes too big. I was afraid to shoot lay-ups because I thought when I lifted my leg to shoot, people could look up my baggy leg hole and see everything. So I sort of stood around. That's when Uncle Harry and Big Jim walked up behind me. "Hey, little Shelb', who's your tailor?" said Big Jim. Uncle Harry added, "Be careful about shooting lay-ups; you can look right up your leg hole and see everything."

I took my spot at the end of the bench. It was a good game until the fourth quarter, when my team began to run away with it. With thirty seconds left to go, I heard the coach's faraway voice call down the bench: "Shelb', get in for Pierson." I wanted to say, "No, that's alright. I'll just sit here a little while longer. Quite frankly, Coach, I haven't been paying very close attention." But I stood up and walked mechanically to the scorer's table, where Uncle Harry winked and waved me into the game.

Somebody passed the ball to somebody else, and something else happened. I think a person dribbled. I hadn't moved from where I had entered the game. I felt like I was watching people play basketball through the wrong end of a telescope.

Suddenly, there was a whistle, and Uncle Harry came running to the stage in front of the scorer's table. "No, no, no," he said, as usual. "Number four-four can't do that. Gets him from behind." Here Uncle Harry put his hands on his hips, bent over backwards, and made a face. "Number five-three shoots two." There was laughter. Everyone was looking at me. I looked down at my jersey. There was number 53. Somebody had fouled me. I hadn't been within thirty feet of the play. I would be shooting free throws. I looked at Uncle Harry. He winked. Big Jim guided me to the line, palmed the ball, held up two fingers, and said, "Little Shelb' will be shooting two, gentlemen."

I missed the first shot. Then I missed the second shot. Another whistle. Big Jim had called a lane violation. I was awarded a third attempt. I missed it. Another whistle. Uncle Harry saw some illegal movement in the lane. A fourth chance. Big Jim leaned over when he handed me the ball, and said, "Sink this one, Little Shelb'. We can't keep doing this all night." I took a deep breath and slung an ugly-looking thing up at the rim. It rattled and rolled in.

Later that year, at Christmas, Uncle Harry handed me a present. It was a nice scrapbook, completely empty, except for the first page. In the center of that first page was a small clipping from the local newspaper about the game just described. At the bottom was the statistics box. The last entry was underlined in red.

Shelby   **No. 53**   **0 0 0 1**   **Total**   **1**

Right below the clip were the handwritten words, "Merry Christmas, from Uncle Harry."

HOW TO FOUL OUT IN SIXTY SECONDS OR LESS

Everyone on the team has a special strength. Use yours.

He was unstoppable, and was considered, at the time, the greatest high school basketball player ever. He went on to distinguish himself at the college and professional levels. Graybeards still say he had the best jump shot in history. But in the process of playing his way into a chapter of basketball history, this star of stars helped Eddie Flynn become one of its more interesting footnotes.

Flynn played for a rival team in the star's conference. Flynn had heard of the star. The star had not heard of Flynn. It's no wonder. Flynn had never started a game in his life. He seldom played, but when he did, he was a delight to watch. In those rare instances when his team was either so far ahead or so far behind that Flynn's presence on the floor would do no harm, Eddie became the whole show. It didn't matter whom he was assigned to guard; he guarded the person with the ball. It didn't matter what plays the coach instructed him to run; he ran his own.

A local announcer once saw Eddie play and said the kid had so much energy, his nickname ought to be Eveready. It stuck. Eveready Eddie Flynn charged up the crowds and his teammates, and it was the purest kind of shame that the boy had absolutely no talent. But three games into the month of December, Eveready Eddie would make himself a legend against one of basketball's greatest talents.

The star was the highest scorer in the state. He averaged forty-one points per game in a tough conference. Nobody could stop him. So the coach, in preparing for the game, decided on a plan. Eddie Flynn was at the center of it.

In the locker room before the game, nerves were raw. Everyone was quiet as the coach called out the starting five. Heads snapped up when the last name called was Eddie Flynn's.

The coach explained his plan. The team would go man-to-man and Flynn would take the legend. "I don't care if he goes to the bathroom, Eddie, I want you with him." Eddie just sat there with a stupid grin on his face. Coach reiterated his defensive plan. "I want you on him like a jockstrap."

The rest of the team thought the coach had gone temporarily insane. He'd just chosen to defend the greatest player in the state with possibly the worst. It made no sense. Then the coach explained himself.

"I want you to foul him," he said to Eddie, looking right into the kid's eyes. "I want you to foul him if he even thinks of taking a shot." Coach straightened up and walked around the room slowly. "I ain't saying to hurt him. I'm just sayin' he better not make the shot. Understand?" Eddie's smile broadened. He understood.

The first foul came before any time was off the clock. As soon as the tip headed in the star's direction, Eddie stuck his foot out and tripped him. Eddie held his hand up proudly and faced the scorer's table. He looked up into the stands and found his mom. Pride showed in her beaming face.

The second foul came fifteen seconds later when the celebrity stole the ball and headed in for the lay-up. If someone told me today that the kid still bore a mark on his forearm twenty-five years later, I'd believe him. Eddie smacked him so hard going for the ball that the contact rang out like a shot. Eddie held up his hand and stole a glance at the coach. Coach nodded his approval and gave him an encouraging wink. Eddie was pumped.

Fouls three and four came on the full-court press. Both times, Eddie and his assignment faced each other on the inbounds pass, and both times Eddie knocked the kid into the bleachers. His fifth foul came off a jump shot. This is the one that Eddie's memory plays in slow motion to this day. The star rises high, both arms fully extended over his head. Eddie rises with him inch for inch and comes within a millisecond of stuffing the great one. Eddie swats the ball and it flies deep into the stands. Fans yell "Rejection!" But the referee blew the foul and said Eddie got the arm.

It was Eddie's greatest performance, yet only fifty-four seconds had ticked off the clock. The star, so shaken by Eddie's early play, finished with a season low of thirty-four points. Eddie took the credit. Two weeks later, Eddie received a letter from the state high school league telling him that his performance against one of history's greatest ballplayers broke the all-time state record for fouling out in the shortest time in history. The star's records have all been eclipsed. But Eddie Flynn's record still stands, unbroken.

THANKSGIVING

There is something new to be grateful for every year.

The aroma of roasting turkey and the gathering of near and distant relatives makes me want to play basketball. It is simple cause-and-effect stuff. In other words, if you are like the folks in my family, Thanksgiving has always been another excuse to put the basketball in your cousin's face. The tradition is a family treasure passed down through the ages, and its adherents faithfully practice its distinct elements.

1. Ascertainment: All adults sit in the living room and ascertain how tall the children have or have not grown. They say things like "Sarah's middle kid will be a small forward or two guard." I grew nine inches between Thanksgivings once, and the

adults ascertained that I would eventually be 6'10". Unfortunately, those were the last inches I grew. The prediction ended up about a foot off.

The standard for ascertainment was Uncle Herb. Uncle Herb was the tallest member of the family, and had played ball in the '50s. All the ballplayers in the family wanted to be taller than Uncle Herb. One year, somebody ascertained that my Aunt Betty's youngest son would be the first to do it. When the boy stuck on 5'1" for two years straight, he stopped showing up at Thanksgiving.

Nobody ever ascertained that my cousin Phillip would end up 6'9". What a waste. The guy would come to Thanksgiving and spend the evening looking through my father's arrowhead collection. He was the only one of us to get a full-ride scholarship, but it was for being smart. He could dunk, but didn't care to. When we would beg him, he would say, "Why should I?" We all hated him. All eighty-one inches of him.

2. Dinner: After the final stages of ascertainment, which includes guessing how tall all the infants will

eventually be, we eat. Unlike other families at the holiday table, we don't waste any time. We eat a lot and we eat it quick, so we can move on to the next stage of the tradition.

3. The Moving of the Cars: Most of us gained our first driving experiences this way. Adults who have to unload hot dishes and carrot Jell-O always park their cars somewhere around the free-throw line, and then the rest of the adults pull in behind. No basketball can be played until all the cars are moved out of the driveway. Several generations of my family are experts at backing up.

4. Choosing Sides: This is the most difficult part of the tradition, and the one that leads most often to family feuds. The first problem is that everyone wants to play, everyone wants to start, and no one wants the fat guy. The other problem is that everyone wants to be on Uncle Jim's team.

   Uncle Jim was All-World and is the LeBron James of our family. He plays only as hard as he has to, and he makes sure everyone on his team scores. He usually ends up on Thanksgiving with about a thousand assists. Everyone in my family wants to grow up to be just like Uncle Jim. Except this year, Uncle Jim shows up and he's the fat guy.

5. The Attire: Generally, we ruin our good clothes. Flannel trousers take on an unforgettable aroma when soaked with sweat. One time, my Uncle Frank took a pass at the top of the key, brushed past a defending nephew, hooked his sweater on the boy's watch, and by the time he got to the basket, the sweater had unraveled so it looked like a dickey. Younger players sometimes show up wearing basketball gear—sweats and high-tops. That's usually a mistake. In my family, sweats and high-tops have never beaten flannels and wingtips.

6. The Game: It is played to 100 by ones, win by two. No game has ever been called because of darkness. Some of our best games were played under such extreme conditions of darkness that you had to keep score by the sound. The game is a mixture of serious, take-no-prisoners basketball and high comedy. The comedy usually comes in

just after the point of complete exhaustion, when the game features a marked increase in hugging and tackling fouls.

But for the first hour or so, it is as good a game of basketball as you can see in a driveway. Family reputations are made and destroyed here. Legitimate stars have been born here, and borne away. Family rivalries persist and Thanksgiving Day dynasties are built and toppled. Old traditions are lived out and new ones started.

Like this year. The stars of the game were two cousins named Bernie and Max, who put it in the face of the biggest and best, high-tops and wingtips alike. And to think, just five years ago, nobody even bothered to ascertain just how tall Bernice and Maxine would grow.

HIS FATHER'S EYES

There is one great game in everyone.

The following story is not my own. I first heard this account when I was eleven. I have heard it told many times since then. You may have heard it before, too.

The boy had come out for the team every year. And, every year, against all bets, he made the team. But just barely. He had little talent, but he worked hard. That alone made him an asset, if only at practice. In the four years he'd played for the high school team, he had accumulated something short of nine minutes of total playing time. His high game was two points. It really didn't seem to matter much to him. In the shadows of the better ballplayers seemed, after four years, the place he wanted to play.

Toward the tail end of his senior year, in a game against a conference rival, something happened that catapulted this boy into the ranks of basketball legend. And, to this day, only a few people understand the facts behind it.

At the half, the boy's team was down by nineteen. The conference title was on the line. The coach was fuming at his players and slamming the clipboard against the lockers. The coach's display was interrupted by the principal of the school, who drew the coach aside and whispered to him. The coach turned to the team and sent them up to the court to shoot around, but he asked the boy to remain in the locker room.

The coach brought the boy aside and sat him down on a bench. Quietly he began, "Son, you have to go home. Your father has passed away." The boy was quiet for a moment as he stared at the floor. As the coach put his hand on the boy's shoulder, the young man lifted his head. "Coach, I'd like to stay," he said. "And," he added, "if you can, I'd like to play." The coach sent the boy up to shoot with the rest of the team and contemplated his course. It was a very important game, but the boy's request, under these circumstances, seemed impossible to deny.

The coach told none of the other players about the boy's father, and the second half began as the first had ended. The boy's team, with the boy on the bench, continued to drop further and further behind. By the end of the third quarter, the opposition had stretched the lead to twenty-eight. The coach, feeling he could do no worse, put the boy in to start the fourth quarter.

From the moment he first touched the ball until the end of the game, the boy played as he had never played before. From somewhere deep within, the boy called up moves and passes and shots he had never before used. His speed dazzled the boys who tried to guard him. He leaped high over the pack to pull down rebound after rebound. Each time the boy touched the ball he put on a clinic. Each time he shot, from wherever he shot, long or short, the ball dropped through, touching nothing but net, and not much of it at that. With one minute left in the game, the boy had singlehandedly closed the gap and brought his team to a tie.

The other team brought the ball up court and set up in a keep-away half-court offense. The object was to hold the ball for the last shot, work a pass into the big man in the middle, and take the lead with only a few seconds left on the clock. Six seconds left, and the pass went to the middle, but the boy was there. He broke first wide, then to the middle. The defense fell back quickly and took away the middle. As the clock ticked away its last second, the boy let fly with a thirty-foot jump shot, and it was perfect. The boy was carried around the gymnasium on the shoulders of the boys in whose shadows he'd played for so many years.

Down in the locker room, after the tumult had subsided, and the shouting had calmed to simple smiles and handshakes, the coach approached the boy, who sat alone now at his locker. The boy was crying. "I have never in my life," said the coach, "seen an exhibition of basketball skill like the one you put on tonight. Why in the world did you play like that tonight, of all nights?"

The boy wiped his eyes with the back of his hand and straightened up to look at the coach. "Coach," he said, "did you ever meet my dad?"

"No," said the coach, "I don't believe I ever did. Why?"

"My dad was blind, Coach. And, this was the first game he ever saw me play."

AUNT BETTY: THE AGELESS ANTAGONIST

She embodied the notion of pardonable prejudice.

She was always the smartest basketball mind in the family. That was her assessment, anyway. And it was hard to argue the point. Few coaches I know have a better grasp on team defense, when to change tempo, when to call time-outs, and when not to. She was the only one in the family who sat in the stands and, instead of screaming at the coach to do something, anything, she'd shout out specific advice: "Attack the entry pass, the guard is cutting your defense to ribbons! Get out of that one-three-one—that baseline guy is killing you! Penetrate and kick—start playing team offense."

You knew Aunt Betty was having an effect when the assistant coaches, and then the head coach, would look up in the stands to locate the ageless sage. And as a coach in the stands, she was also every referee's worst nightmare. She didn't simply complain about any call that went against her team. That wasn't her style. She loved basketball, and she believed referees facilitated good basketball and never impeded it. It was her view that a referee wasn't there to decide who wins and loses. If a referee blew a call, she let the referee know, loudly and in a way designed to humiliate. That was all pretty standard stuff.

But when she saw a referee take over a game, she became a madwoman—a fire-breathing, fully involved force of nature. And what made her madness sanity itself is that everyone in the building, including the offending referees, knew she was right.

Aunt Betty always took a seat in the bleachers nearest the floor. Coaches and referees would enter the gym, their eyes scanning the first five rows from the floor. The average fan would never have noticed, but we all knew they were looking, with dread, for Aunt Betty's face.

She had had quite a career, but in her eighty-third year of life, she began to slow down. Her acute criticism and verbosity were undiminished by age, but she went to fewer games. A hundred a season was the most she could manage as an octogenarian. And there was another change. The Indiana High School League had passed a new regulation. It stated that it was unsportsmanlike for fans to criticize the play, the coaching, or the officiating of a game. Anyone who failed to refrain from such behavior after having been warned was subject to removal. It was up to the official to decide whether the criticism was partisan. If it was, a technical foul could be assessed against the team the offending fan was rooting for. In other words, Aunt Betty was now an often-unwanted sixth man.

Last year, she turned eighty-nine. Uncle Bob stopped going to the games with her. She had not mellowed with age, she had gotten worse, and after more than sixty years of marriage, Uncle Bob decided to watch the games on television or listen to them on the radio. If the announcers' microphones were courtside, he could hear his wife's voice as clearly as if he were by her side. He just wouldn't have to suffer the stares of pity for the embarrassed man standing in Aunt Betty's shadow.

Toward the end of that season, there came a game of the ages between two teams whose rivalry stretched back to Aunt Betty's teen years. Her team, by Betty's own estimation, was outmatched by the competition's starting five. As the game progressed, the two teams traded leads, and Aunt Betty was quieter than normal. Those around her began to think she had reformed, or that in her dotage had lost her intensity. Nothing could have been further from the truth. She was just waiting for her opening. It presented itself with only twenty-eight seconds left on the clock. A point guard split defenders, faked a kick-out pass, threw off a defender, and softly banked a lay-up. A one-point lead. Fifteen seconds left. Aunt Betty went to work. She stood in her third-row seat in the bleachers and screamed at the referee that the boy now dribbling across the ten-second line had carried the ball in a crossover move. Her tirade was so great that not only spectators and referees, but also several of the players, slowed down to watch the spectacle.

She cut a path down to the floor and verbally attacked the referee nearest her sideline. She called him every name she could think of, using the most colorful language she could muster. The referee called an official time-out. Now Aunt Betty was on the court itself and was driving her finger into the striped chest of the official. He put both hands on her shoulders and walked her back off the court and warned her that another outburst like that would result in a technical foul.

Aunt Betty wasn't to be placated by what she called "a pipsqueak." The official did the only thing he could. He gave her a technical foul and ejected her from the gymnasium. Guards came from all corners and walked her to the exit. She was agile at eighty-nine, but for this show she developed a halting gait, slow and jerky. The crowd was on her side. The nerve of a referee to T-bone an eighty-nine-year-old lady, eject her from the premises, and, to top it off, award the requisite two foul shots to the other team. The point guard who had been accused of palming the ball on the crossover dribble went to the line with his team down by one. The first shot was all net. The score was now tied, and only four seconds remained on the game clock.

Aunt Betty reached her car, having shaken off the arthritic bit of drama, started the engine, and turned on the radio. She heard the announcer say that the guard was at the line, going through his routine for the final shot—a shot that would, in all likelihood, give the game to his team, if he could only make it. Aunt Betty sat stone-faced and heard the announcer say that the ball was in the air. It hit the back of the rim and bounced straight up, then back toward the cylinder. The moment was frozen in time. It hit the rim and bounced up again, and the announcer let it be known that the ball had touched nearly every part of the goal. It finally settled and rattled down through the net. The team now had a one-point lead, and in the four remaining seconds, the opposition was unable to get the ball down the court for a shot. The buzzer sounded and the game was over.

A technical foul, brought on by the tirade of a woman pushing ninety, had decided the game. Aunt Betty sat in the car, her breathing heavy and her head bowed. She stared down in silence for a few minutes, and then she slowly raised her head. Aunt Betty began to smile. As she pulled out of the parking lot and listened to the announcer explain that a deranged old lady had disrupted the game, attacked a referee, and violated the state high school athletic regulation against criticism, resulting in a two-shot technical foul, her smile turned into a smirk, the smirk into a chuckle, and eventually she let out a full-bellied laugh. What only one other person in the gymnasium knew, what Aunt Betty would never confess, was that the point guard at the line with a two-shot technical—the one she accused of carrying the ball on the dribble, the one who won the game—was her grandson.

THE WRONG SIDE OF THE TRACKS

Sometimes it takes a while to learn the lesson.

Tina Brookman was the Armistice Day Queen and the daughter of Mr. and Mrs. Willard Brookman, owners of Brookman's Fine Men's Clothes.

Lonnie Thomas was an all-state senior forward and the son of Mrs. Mary Thomas, a cook at The Oasis, "Delaware County's Singular Dining Experience."

Tina was a cheerleader and Lonnie was a ballplayer, and the two had pledged to love each other until eternity, and had sealed their love with the exchange of letter jackets. Tina wore Lonnie's, but Lonnie refused to wear Tina's, saying only that it didn't fit.

Tina and Lonnie were in love and spent much of their time talking about their lives together. They talked of marriage and children. They planned their futures and talked about going to the same college. He would play basketball and get a job and she could be a cheerleader or a mother. It didn't matter, as long as they were together.

But everyone knew nothing would come of it. Lonnie was from a section of town called Morningside. Folks in Morningside lived in small houses and drove old cars. Tina was from Elmhurst. Because of that, Tina had money, station, and prospects. Being from Morningside, Lonnie had no prospects, save basketball. No one from Elmhurst had ever married anyone from Morningside. Mr. Brookman hoped that would never change. He hated Morningside and the class of people who lived there. He hated Lonnie most of all.

When Mr. Brookman forbade Tina from ever seeing Lonnie again, Tina and her father stopped talking. Where once there had been a deep, affectionate love, there was now cold ugliness. Mr. Brookman believed he could yet breathe life into the relationship. But it couldn't be done as long as Lonnie was in the picture.

Lonnie took everything in stride. His early struggles had taught him toughness. It made him attractive to Tina, and it made him one of the best ballplayers in the state. Now, with tournament time approaching, Lonnie was about to take center stage for the first time in his life, and Mr. Willard Brookman could not prevent that.

Three days before the sectional tournament, Lonnie stopped into Brookman's Fine Men's Clothes to buy a new tie. Everybody on the team had to wear the same tie to the tournament, and Brookman's was the supplier. Mr. Brookman saw Lonnie in his three-way mirror. That's when he did it.

It happened so fast, and without so much as a second's thought. Willard picked up a seventy-five dollar pair of cufflinks, walked to where Lonnie's jacket was hanging, and slipped the box into the pocket. He then placed a call to the police. The squad car pulled up just as Lonnie was leaving. He was stopped and searched, and the cufflinks were discovered. He tried to tell the police he didn't know how they had gotten into his pocket, but the cops said they'd heard it all before. Mr. Brookman pressed charges. Lonnie's mom couldn't make bail, so Lonnie went to jail to await trial.

The shock was felt everywhere. Selfishly, the coaches wondered what they would do now. Tina couldn't believe Lonnie would have stolen anything, but her father saw him do it, and despite everything that had happened between them, Tina couldn't imagine that her father was lying. Elmhurst folks talked amongst themselves about how things like this always happened with kids from Morningside.

Two weeks passed, and Lonnie remained in jail. A public defender got a court date set, but it was two months away. Tina was forbidden from visiting Lonnie. Meanwhile, the team made it through the sectional, squeaked through the regional, and had gotten lucky to survive the semi-state. The state finals were coming up the next weekend, and townsfolk were getting edgy about trying to take on the state's finest teams down in the capitol city without the help of the state's best forward, Lonnie Thomas. As a result, a movement began to build.

It started quietly. One fan talking to another. Then they held a couple of meetings. They invited a lawyer and a judge to the next. The president of the Chamber of Commerce, whose son played center, also showed up. Their objective was to get Lonnie out of jail in time to play in the state tournament. They arrived at only one solution: They had to get Willard Brookman to drop the charges.

At lunchtime on the Friday before the finals, a group of ten walked into Brookman's Fine Men's Clothes. They made it plain. If the team lost in the state finals, the town would blame Willard, pure and simple. They would take their business over to Kaufman's or the Dapper Dan's. Willard said he'd think about it. That night, he thought of his daughter, and his business, and the high school team. He thought about himself and what he had done.

Saturday morning's paper arrived with the banner headline: BROOKMAN DROPS CHARGES—THOMAS TO PLAY.

Two days later, the team went down to the big barn and brought home the trophy. Lonnie played his finest game ever and was named the tournament's Most Outstanding Player. There had been signs in the crowd. Crude drawings of prison bars. Some kids shouted that Lonnie was a convict and a criminal. It worked against them. Lonnie was tough. More, he knew it wasn't true.

Many years later, at a big family get-together, Willard got up from the table and asked Lonnie to take a walk with him. Outside, a pack of boys and girls were shooting at the basket hanging above the garage door. Lonnie and Mr. Brookman sat down on the patio chairs and watched a while in silence. Then the old man reached over and patted the back of Lonnie's hand and said, "I just wanted to tell you that I'm sorry. I hope someday you'll understand."

As Willard walked away, one of the children jumped onto Lonnie's lap. "Daddy, why is Grandpa crying?"

EXCUSES

There is a downside to talking smack.

"Just don't sit there all day, go find somebody to play with," my mom said. I'd always liked going up to the lakes, but now, at thirteen, the place was sort of boring. Nothing to do. Too young to do fun stuff. Too old to do stupid junk. Nothing to do.

"Go play," she said.

"Nothin' to play," I sighed.

"Play basketball."

Nobody to play with, I told her. Too far to walk. The only court was all the way down at Guy White's house, and there were so many mosquitoes…

"Donald Gilbert Shelby, you get out of this house this very minute."

"I'm going," I said, shuffling through the screen door and dribbling my basketball on the way out. "I'm going."

As I approached the court at Guy White's house, I could see another kid already there shooting around. He didn't look very good, and I quickened my step. I loved playing against guys I could beat.

We shot around awhile without saying a word to each other. We abided by the protocol of never shooting with the other guy's ball. After I was absolutely sure I could beat this guy one-on-one, I said, "Wanna play some?"

"Sure," he said. "Forty by two's?"

"Okay," I said. "First outs."

"Whatever," he said.

The game was over in five minutes. Score: 40-12, my favor. I demolished the guy, but he took it pretty well. He wanted to know if I'd be coming up to the lakes anymore during the summer for a rematch. I told him I wasn't, but I would take him on next year, right here at Guy White's house. We exchanged addresses and telephone numbers and promised to meet again.

During the winter months, the guy called several times.

He bragged that he was getting better. I told him he'd have to. As time wore on toward that next summer, we had talked ourselves into a pretty serious grudge match. The guy said half his family was going to show up for the showdown at Guy White's court. I told him he'd need the help.

On the ride up to the lakes, I told my mom and dad they should come over to Guy White's and watch me teach this kid a few lessons. They both said they'd come, and they'd bring Aunt Betty.

As we approached Guy's house, I could see about a dozen people watching an unfamiliar guy shooting around. I was upset that I'd have to ask this big guy to leave the court while we played our game. By the time we got to the driveway, I realized I wouldn't have to ask him to leave. It was him.

We shot around for a few minutes, and then he said, "You ready?" I told him I was, although I hadn't been feeling myself lately.

"Forty by two's?" he asked.

"Whatever," I said.

He scored the first six baskets unanswered. "What the heck kind of ball is this?" I asked. We were using his.

"MacGregor," he said.

"No wonder," I said, shaking my head.

I scored twice, but he scored four more straight to make it 20-4 at the half. All of his family stood up and applauded. I held my side and walked off the court bent over.

"What's the matter?" he asked.

"It's my gull splatter," I said. "I almost had my gull splatter taken out last year, and it's hurting again." (My father had had a "gull splatter" operation several years back, and when I had come down with a pain in my side about a year earlier, my father had thought it could be the same thing. My mother thought it was the two quarts of Bing cherries I'd had for lunch.)

The second half began with the guy hitting three straight and me sneaking in one lucky one. My wincing increased, and I developed a limp. I was hoping he'd have mercy and call the game, but he was loving it too much.

The game ended 40-10. I whined that it was unfair. The ball was his and it was a MacGregor. I had this pain and this limp. Had I been healthy, with a Voit or a Spalding, I could have won. I told him he was lucky and demanded a rematch for the next year to settle it, best two out of three. He accepted. I stormed off.

My dad, who had seen the whole thing start to finish, put his arm around me and told me he knew it was tough to lose. He said he knew it was tougher to lose after running your mouth about how much better you are than the other guy. He said losing like that required humility, not excuses.

"Now," he said, "I want you to go over there and say these words: 'You really kicked my butt today.'"

"I will not," I snapped.

"Yes, you will," he said. "And you will say, 'You have really improved. Right now, you are better than me.' "

"Why do I have to say that?" I demanded.

"Because it is true and because it is right," my father said.

When I spoke them, my dad's words embarrassed the boy. "Aw," he said, "you had a side-ache and a hurt foot."

"No, I didn't," I said. "You beat me fair and square."

"Thanks," he said. "See ya next summer."

Dad put his arm around me as we silently walked back to the cottage. Even Aunt Betty seemed sensitive to my humiliation. When we got to the driveway, Dad suggested we all go out for a milkshake. Then he leaned down and whispered in my ear, "They tell me milkshakes are just the thing for an ailing gull splatter."

PLAYGROUND BALL

Sometimes it really isn't about winning or losing.

"Let's take our stuff downtown," I said. I tried to sound cocky. We'd held the park court for more than four hours, twenty games or so. The challengers had dispersed, gone home, quit in frustration, saying they had to study, or bail hay, or meet their girlfriends. We were full of ourselves and ready to take on any comers, but there were none left. So, I repeated it. "Let's take our stuff downtown."

That was brazen talk, even for me. We had never been downtown to play ball. We had been downtown shopping with our mothers, and had driven by the playgrounds where the city kids played. It seemed to us a different game, a scarier game, a more serious game. The environment seemed different, too: rims bent, backboards of metal screen, chains on the hoops instead of nets. The balls did not swish through these cylinders. They clanked.

Even though we had never so much as committed a lay-up on one of these courts, we knew about them. Most of what we knew was myth. But it was a mythology based on certain indisputable truths. For instance, it was a well-established and ascertainable fact that Oscar Robertson used to play here. He and a handful of kids from his neighborhood had driven nearly sixty miles for the game. They waited several hours, passing up invitations to play until the dominant local five had held the court through ten games or more. Then, Oscar and his partners, still dressed in street clothes and wingtips, strolled onto the court and beat the champs mercilessly. They said the game went less than five minutes, twenty by ones, and the losers never got the ball past half court.

Oscar was long gone now, having moved far beyond these asphalt courts, but his ghost haunted us yet as we drove into the city. Our cockiness drained away as we pulled within sight of the church behind which stood the fabled court. My first impression was that the rims were much lower than the ones on the courts where we usually played. As we got closer, I began to realize the baskets were regulation; it was just that the players were taller. Even the smaller guys seemed to be spending a lot of time above the rims.

I now wanted to take our stuff back home. We were out of place. We were altogether out of place. We reeked of the country. Moments before, in the car coming down here, we were cool. Now, as we stood watching the city kids, the humiliating realization overtook us. These guys were cool. We were not.

By the time we had sat through three games, some fundamental differences in how we played began to emerge. The most obvious difference was what constituted a foul. Back home, a foul was any physical contact that resulted in a missed shot or a turnover. Here, it seemed, a foul required drawing blood or rendering a player unconscious. Even then, the called foul resulted in an automatic and bitter argument, and sometimes more blood and unconsciousness.

"You next?" one of them finally asked. They turned and looked at us. Nobody smiled, nobody shook hands, nobody introduced himself. We had learned some of their names from watching: Mouse, Robert D., and a brooding guy who looked like James Dean in high-tops named Johnny.

"Who are those other guys?" I asked Mouse, pointing to the two tallest players on their side.

"Chop and J.T. Arthur," answered Mouse with a smile. I stopped breathing. Chop and J.T. Arthur had been great high school stars. Chop had gone on to play some college ball and J.T. had joined the Army and made a name for himself playing basketball in Europe. Now they played eight hours a day on this asphalt. My brother once saw J.T. hold the great George McGinnis scoreless three games running, and court rats who knew such things said Chop was even better than his brother.

The sun was low in the sky when Mouse inbounded to Johnny. Two hours passed before we took our first break. The game was twenty by ones, win by two. The score was tied at something over fifty when we called time. Mouse had gone out with a broken hand at about forty, and a walk-on named Slack more than took his place. Chop and J.T. had dominated under the boards, but we had been unconscious from the outside. We had also taken away their fast break. We had not been able to stop them through the lane, though. All of us were bruised and most of us were bleeding. Our knees and shins ached from the pounding up and down the asphalt. There had been near-brawls at twenty-five and forty-five. When we started the game, there had been five or six people watching. By midnight, more than two hundred ringed the court, perched in trees or standing on top of their cars for a glimpse of the action. Word had traveled. And this night was becoming legendary, with no winners in sight.

The crowd was clearly with the city kids, but basketball people are generous and appreciative. We heard the occasional encouraging word like, "Pretty." Fifteen minutes after the break, the game was over. Robert D. had stripped me of the ball two times down the court, and those two baskets ended it. No one knew the score. The game had been reduced to the simple tallying of "up one." The ball had not cleared the chains on that final shot before we all embraced and fell into a heap on the asphalt. The pile was all laughter, and slapping, and the repeated word, "Man!"

As the emotion subsided and we gathered our stuff to go, J.T. Arthur walked over to us and smiled. He nodded over his shoulder at the dozen or so spectators who had hung around, some of them acting out highlights of the game.

"You know they're gonna talk about this one for a long

time," he said.

"It was a great game," I said.

Chop walked up. "Did you see who was here?" he asked. We hadn't noticed.

"Oscar," he said. Breath momentarily left my body.

"Oscar was here?" I gasped.

"Just left," said Chop. "Said you guys were really something."

The ride home started out in high gear. Much talk of the game and, of course, the fact that Oscar had seen us play. The heady suggestion that he might even know our names. The final moments of the trip turned quiet. The silence was broken when one of us spoke a thought aloud: I wonder, when we grow up, the thought went, will anything happen to make us feel like this again?

"I doubt it," I said. "I very seriously doubt it."

THE SHOWDOWN
WITH SHOWTIME

No matter how good you are, you can be better.

W e had been beaten only once the year before, so this season seemed like the year we would go all the way, especially with the new guy. He had moved into our school system over the summer and all of us had gotten to know him pretty well. He wasn't exactly lovable, but he was spectacular with a basketball. He had seven Division I schools looking, and a couple had made backdoor offers of full-ride scholarships. He was a junior. The other four returning starters were seniors. He'd fit in nicely.

Most of us had never seen a guard play basketball the way he did. He was all over the court, driving, cutting, shooting from short and long. In those days he was considered a hot dog, a showboat. He was a cut above Cousy because he was much more athletic. He was more like Michael Jordan, before anyone could have dreamed up Michael Jordan. The kid was playing on the crest of a new wave of basketball. We were excited to have him on our team, but we soon learned that we would be playing most of our basketball in his wake.

Our coach had built one of the best winning records in the state by putting teams on the court, year after year, that played as units. We had never been blessed with a star, but we won a lot of games. The coach believed you could create a sum greater than the total of its parts if you worked as a team. He loved teamwork. He made us love it. The new kid wasn't so impressed.

There was difficulty from the first day of practice. When we ran the full-court weave drill, he managed to get himself into position to always take the shot. Instead of passing it off to one of the other two drivers for the lay-up, he'd pop from twenty feet. Whenever we'd practice our motion offense, the motion would stop when the ball got into his hands. He would shoot. Problem was, he'd usually hit. Our attitudes began to smell and our teamwork stunk worse. But the new kid didn't notice. He was the only person I ever met in all my years of playing basketball who kept count of every basket he scored—in practice.

When the season started, we lost the first six games. The new guy, on the other hand, posted some remarkable numbers in those games. He led the conference with a thirty-five points-per-game average. He was the talk of the state, and the season wasn't a month old. The school had to rope off an area behind the scorer's table just for the college scouts. Newspaper reporters showed up in droves and crowded the locker room for interviews. The rest of us were left unmolested by the press corps. The one thing the reporters kept missing was the fact that the year before we had gone almost undefeated without the guy and now we couldn't win a game with him. We decided to act.

The next day at study hall, the four seniors went to the cage to talk to the coach.

"Coach," we said, "we're tired of losing, tired of the new guy not running the plays, tired of him getting all the credit, and tired of being a support system for his road to glory." We told him we wanted to change things, and quick.

Coach told us he was glad we had come, but said there was little he could do.

"I can't sit him down," he said. "He is a brilliant ballplayer. If I were to sit him down, I'd have hell to pay. And he won't listen to me. I've drilled those plays into his head since the first day of practice. He just wants to do it alone."

"Then what can we do?" we asked.

"Let him do it alone," answered the coach.

"What do you mean?" we asked.

"You can't score without the ball," he said. "And since the rules say that you can't inbound the ball to yourself, somebody has got to give it to you. If nobody gives you the ball, you can't do jack. Now, go back to class."

We kept the coach's thoughts to ourselves, but we perfected our game plan. Since the new guy played guard with me, we decided the center or one of the two forwards would always take the ball out and inbound to me. From then on, it was simple. We would just play keep-away. Four against five.

Two nights later, we played our first game under the new plan, and it was wonderful. The place was filled with spectators and scouts and news people from all over. By the end of the first half, the new guy had scored two points on a steal. At halftime, the coach was late coming down into the locker room because the scouts had cornered him near the bench, demanding to know what was going on. Coach just shrugged and said everybody has an off night once in a while.

We won the game. The reporters left without conducting any interviews. One of the scouts spent some time talking to the center's parents. We won six of our next seven ballgames. It was a tumultuous period. The kid went from crazy anger to depression to anger again. He threatened to quit. His parents threatened to go to the school board.

Then, one day, we saw the kid mope into the cage. Less than a minute later, he walked out smiling. None of us knew what had happened, but it worked.

Before the next game, the coach told the four seniors to call off our freeze-out and include the kid in the offense. That night, and for every game thereafter, we played as a team. Even though the kid usually led in scoring, it was balanced. And we kept winning. The reporters came back, as did the scouts, and some of them even talked to us. Eventually, the kid went on to college, and then to the pros in the second round.

A couple years later I stopped by the cage to talk with the coach and I asked him, among other things, what had happened that turned the kid around. He said the boy came into the cage and said he was the best player that had ever gone to this school and that there was nothing he couldn't do on the basketball court. The coach said he looked at the boy and said simply, "You can't lead the conference in assists."

The kid proved him wrong.

LONG DISTANCE

Reaping what you sow, at half-court.

I don't know how he managed it, but Rickie Otis figured out a way to get a permanent excuse from the last period of the day. That gave him a full hour before practice to dress and goof around in the gym. Rickie was long on energy, but shy on real basketball talent. He had no offense, but his defense was something to behold. It was not scrappy; it was frenetic. He was only good for about three minutes at any one stretch. By the end of that span he had either exhausted himself or fouled out of the game.

But it was the last period of the day that made him famous. He would come down to the gym early every day. He always began the way the coach had instructed. First, right-handed shots from five feet, then left-handed shots from the opposite side. After fifty or so shots, he would move, as the coach had instructed him, to fifteen feet and repeat the process.

Coach believed that if you were going to be excused from your last class to dress for practice, you should use it to good advantage. No funny business. Coach hated funny business, and that meant a prohibition against taking any shot you would not shoot in a game. But after a while, Rickie would lose interest in the coach's shooting routine and begin heaving up long-distance shots from three-quarter court.

If Coach caught you attempting shots like this, he would threaten to bench you for the rest of your life. "What the hell kind of a percentage shot is that when you can't even hit a simple jumper from fifteen?" he would yell from the shadow of the bleachers. But that didn't stop Rickie. Halfway through the hour he would get bored and start talking to himself, pretending that he was both the radio announcer and the ballplayer that the announcer was talking about. You could hear him all the way up in study hall.

"Otis with the ball off the inbounds pass. Five seconds to go, Otis's team down by two. Three, two…Otis with a desperation shot! It's…in! I can't believe it! Rickie Otis drops the game-winner from three-quarter court. The crowd is going wild!"

Rickie might repeat that call fifty times in an afternoon—or as many times as he could get away with before Coach discovered the funny business. Rickie just loved that scenario. He never expected that it would eventually result in the best moment of his life.

The night we all played in the final game of the regional tournament, Rickie was used sparingly. Everybody was pumped, and Rickie's special defensive skills weren't needed until the close of the first half. We had gotten down in the last minutes, and the coach wanted us to go to the dressing room with the lead. Coach always wanted to be ahead at halftime. With eight seconds to go and the team trailing by one point, Rickie took the inbounds pass, wheeled on the spot, and heaved up that three-quarter-court bomb. *Swish.* The crowd was nuts. It seemed like a long time before the buzzer sounded. Coach had steam coming out of his ears.

In the dressing room, he slammed his clipboard onto the cold concrete floor. It echoed down the long row of lockers behind us.

"What the hell kind of shot was that?" he demanded to know. An underclassman whispered, "A long one." Coach's eyes burned holes in the kids. "Otis," he finally said, in a trembling voice, "you had eight seconds on the clock and you threw up some stupid dream shot when you had four players all over the court closer to the basket. You had the time, the passing lanes, and the people. You blew it. I'd rather come down here at halftime behind than earn a lead that way. You owe me laps, buster. You owe me stairs. You owe me laps and stairs, with a weight vest."

Rickie just sat there looking down at his shoelaces. We hurt for him. Tomorrow Rickie would be running the forty steps up to the top of the gym and back down the next aisle with a twenty-pound weight vest on. There were sixteen of those aisles. While we all felt bad for Rickie, we understood the coach's logic. The shootaround before the start of the second half was quiet. When play got underway, Rickie was on the bench. Well, not actually on the bench. He was on the medicine box on the far end of the bench. The student manager was sitting closer to the coach than Rickie was.

The game went on much the way it had in the first half. We traded buckets. It was an exciting game, but we couldn't pull away, and neither could they. We were down by three with about thirty seconds left when someone stole a pass and made an easy lay-up to bring us to within one. They brought the ball up, tried to hold it, and made a foolish pass that bounced off the center's foot under their basket. Our ball. Four seconds left. Coach calls for a time-out.

As we headed over to the huddle, Coach walked to the end of the bench and bent down over Rickie. He whispered in Rickie's ear for the whole time-out. When the horn blew, Rickie went to the scorer's table and checked in. He took a position at three-quarter court.

Before the ref handed the inbounder the ball, Rickie looked over his shoulder at the coach. Coach's face didn't change. He just nodded. The crowd grew still. The ball came in to Rickie. He shook his man inside and broke out toward the sideline. The crowd rose to its feet as one. I looked up from the bench and saw Rickie's face. He was talking. No, he was announcing.

"It's Otis," I heard him say. "Three, two…he lets it fly!" And he did. The ball arched up toward the rafters and drifted like a balloon. You could see the seams of the ball rotating evenly. Somewhere in mid-flight the buzzer sounded. Shortly after that, the ball reached the backboard, kissed it hard, and sunk itself into the center of the hoop. The crowd poured onto the floor and we poured onto Rickie. We raised him to our shoulders, and the fight song was chorused in his honor.

Coach turned quietly from the tumult and walked into the locker room, never to discuss the event again. I never learned whether the coach had ordered Rickie to take the shot or whether it was Rickie's doing. Rickie never said, and nobody had the nerve to ask the coach. All I know is that at the next practice, Rickie ran the stairs with the weight vest on his chest and a smile on his face.

SUMMERTIME

You never know who's watching.

Not long ago, a guy named Johnny McCoy told me something that startled me. He said, "I want to thank you for keeping me on the right track." I didn't know what he was talking about. I had known Johnny many, many years ago. We were both ballplayers, years apart. I asked him to explain, and he told me a story about summer.

Summer, he said, is a basketball player's off-season. It's a time to get away from the discipline of practice and the watchful eye of the coaches. Sometimes, he said, you can get too far away. "That's what happened to me one summer," he said.

Johnny had ended his junior year with a scrapbook full of clippings and a wall full of hardware. "Work hard this summer," the coach had told Johnny. "And Johnny," the coach added, "stay in line." That was coach-talk for avoiding things other people might try.

Johnny passed his first month of the summer playing ball in the church league. But the schedule only ran through the end of June. When July rolled around, Johnny faced it with a mixture of relief and uneasiness. He was relieved that he could think about something else besides basketball for a while and uneasy because without basketball he felt like he was drifting out of line.

It started simply enough. A summertime party. Some guys brought beer. Some of his teammates were there and they had a few. Johnny had a couple. That weekend, there was another party and more beer. Some guys brought smokes. At first, Johnny resisted the cigarettes. Drinking was one thing, he thought, but smoking was not cool. By August he was smoking a pack a day. By the time that summer ended, Johnny had earned a reputation among his newfound friends for being able to knock back a case of beer in a weekend.

When school started in September, the first thing the coaches noticed was that Johnny was heavier. When he showed up at pick-up games, everyone could see how far out of shape he'd gotten. Second-string guys he'd dominated the year before handled him easily. "What's going on?" the coaches wanted to know. "Nothin's going on," was Johnny's answer. "I'll be okay by the time the season starts." He made a promise to himself to quit drinking and smoking.

After the first hard workout of the season, Johnny needed a smoke to settle his stomach. I'll cut down, he told himself. "But I didn't," he told me. "I just worked harder in practice to get in shape and kept on doing what I was doing. I convinced myself I could play well and still do those things."

One night after practice, Johnny had a few beers with some of his new friends. On the way home he drove his truck into the ditch in front of his folks' farm. His dad found some beer bottles on the floor of the truck and the ashtray filled with butts. Johnny told his dad they belonged to someone else. His dad wanted it to be true, so he believed his son. Nobody but Johnny knew what was happening.

The first home game of Johnny's senior year was a sellout. Fans who had spent their summer looking forward to Johnny's final season poured in from three counties. It was a big night, and Johnny had been drinking. He played terribly. He ended the game on the bench. It was a subdued crowd that filed out of the gym that night.

"I sat in the locker room that night and blamed everyone else for how I played. All I wanted to do was get into my truck and drink a few beers," he told me. But that was about to change.

"As I walked out of the locker room, there was a kid, about seven or eight years old, standing there, waiting for me. He just stood there looking at me. It was like he couldn't talk. He handed me a pencil and piece of paper. He wanted my autograph. This kid wanted my autograph. I signed my name and handed him the paper and pencil. As I walked away, the kid said, 'Hey, Johnny, I'm going to grow up and be just like you.'

"Do you remember that?" he asked me.

"Yes," I said. "I still have the autograph."

Johnny drove straight home that night. He said he never smoked again and that it was a very long time before he drank another beer.

"I guess I just wanted to thank you for being that little kid," Johnny said.

"Thanks for being my hero," I said.

NORTH WALNUT STREET FIELD HOUSE REVISITED

You can never go back, but you'll never forget.

Early January, 1965. Muncie, Indiana. A heavy, wet snow is falling outside the North Walnut Street Field House, the third-largest high school gymnasium in the country. Inside, eight thousand spectators are watching the final game of the county tournament. Doug DeBord is calling the game for the local radio station, and on the floor I am having the game of my life.

I am not simply playing better than usual. I am playing like somebody else. The ball is going into the basket almost every time I shoot it. From time to time, I catch myself looking over at the bench after hitting another shot, smiling. Our coach thought it sinful to smile while playing basketball. He forgave me this time. He was smiling, too. Nobody could believe it.

That game has never left me. I believe I think of that game for a little while every day. Some people might find it odd that after more than forty years a grown man would allow himself such juvenile conceit. But it is necessary to understand that, with the exception of building my family, my life never got better than that night in the North Walnut Street Field House. Nothing I've done equals that one winter evening when I scored twenty-five points and made the all-county first team and entered the Indiana State High School record book with the most field goals made in the county tournament. I can't imagine doing anything else that would make me feel that way again. And so it has been with a real sense of purpose that I have pursued that memory, in a tangible way, for the past twenty-five years.

Let me explain.

The next school day after the tournament, the coach invited me to the cage and said, "Shelb', sit down and listen to this." He turned the play switch on the old Wollensak tape recorder, and from the speakers came the familiar sound of the crowd and the voice of Doug DeBord. The coach had gotten a recording of the radio broadcast of that game. For the next hour and a half I listened. It is the sound of that broadcast that has filled my daydreams. When the tape ran out, the coach put it in a box and told me to go back to class. Despite my efforts, I never saw or heard the tape again.

Twenty years ago, I began a search for that game tape by calling the coach himself. He hadn't seen it. He thought it belonged to the radio station. A call to the radio station turned up no tape. Calls to the play-by-play announcers, his assistants, the city librarian, the high school league historian, basketball referees and junkies turned up nothing. For a week or so a year, every year, I would set out to find that tape. Every time I would start with the coach.

Three weeks after my fiftieth birthday, I was visiting relatives in Indiana and I mentioned my efforts to track down the tape. I spouted off that I would pay a thousand bucks to anyone who could come up with the tape. My niece Kim said she'd take on the project, and I bid her good luck. I knew I had exhausted every possible avenue and I was sadly confident she'd never find the tape.

Three days later she called and said she had found it. I couldn't believe it.

"Where?" I asked.

"Oh," she said, with a smile in her voice, "your coach had it all the time. He said it was in a box he hadn't looked in." A headline flashed across my brain: ECSTATIC SHELBY MURDERS OLD COACH.

I told my wife the tape had been found, and all she could say was, "The thousand-dollar tape?" As the tape made its way to me, I found myself suddenly unsure I wanted to hear it. Because as long as that game was locked up in a reel of tape nobody could find, my mind had been free to invent a game unbound by the fetters of reality or humility. It was a game where I was at my best, where my world was at its best—inside the North Walnut Street Field House. There was a chance I'd hear the tape and be disappointed. There was also the chance the tape would make me feel seventeen and pure again. And if that happened, a thousand dollars was peanuts.

When the tape arrived, it was on a seven-inch reel. It took me weeks to find a tape recorder that would play it. I set it up in the basement and I waited until my wife and children had all left the house to do chores or visit friends. I didn't want them to hear it. Not just yet. They'd heard about this tape for so many years. Now I was worried that it wouldn't sound as impressive as I had remembered. When they were gone, I set up the player and put on headphones.

The sound began abruptly. I heard the crowd. It is hard to mistake the sound of eight thousand people in one of the biggest basketball barns in the country. It was a sound, I realized, that I had never forgotten, that I had unknowingly chased. Then came the voice of the announcer saying, "Live from the North Walnut Street Field House, the final game of the Delaware County tournament, pitting the Redbirds of Royerton High School against the Daleville Broncos. And here's the starting lineups…" As the names were called off, I began to drift back to 1965. I saw the faces of every boy on both teams. I wondered if any of them, now grown men, ever think of that game the way I had done for almost forty years.

I was playing point guard that night, as I had every game since joining varsity. I had averaged just over ten points a game for the season, but I led the team in assists. My job was to get the ball to the bigger, better ballplayers. But this was likely the last game of my high school career, and an assistant coach (my history teacher) grabbed my arm in the huddle before we took the floor for the tip and said, "Shelb', shoot the ball tonight." No one had ever given me that permission, and I took his words to heart.

At the tip-off, I took the ball across the ten-second line and fired. Good. I was no longer listening to a tape recording. I was listening to the highlight of my youth. I ended up with twenty-five that night, still the record in Delaware County for most field goals made in a final game.

When the tape ended, I sat in the chair in the basement with my headphones on, the tape flapping on the reel-to-reel recorder. I was untroubled by responsibility, bills, work, war, politics, and age. I was seventeen again, in our traveling black uniforms, in the North Walnut Street Field House, playing my final game, an assistant coach telling me to shoot the ball, and Doug DeBord at the microphone calling the best game I would ever play.

I knew my wife and daughters would be home soon, and that I'd be old again. The old man, with his stories of Indiana basketball and hardwood glory, would be sitting where they had left him hours earlier, but what a trip he'd taken. My first impulse was to rewind the tape and play the broadcast for my family, so they could hear for themselves that it hadn't all been just talk, that I had been somebody once. But I knew what I had once been was of little importance now. Listening to the tape would be, for them, mere nostalgia. What mattered to them was who I was today. I boxed up the tape and haven't listened to it since. But I see that game—my youth in my heart—every single day.

WAR GAMES

And the band played on.

Editor's Note: This was written on June 22, 1991, the day the first Gulf War began.

Who knows what will have occurred by the time you read this. I am writing from a newsroom frantic with reporters. Another missile has hit Tel Aviv, and this time there are deaths. I have been busy gathering the information on the casualties, making sure our reporter in Tel Aviv is alive and able to report on what he's seen. And I have been trying to find time to write this. It's very important to me that I write this today—to write about basketball, even in the midst of death and uncertainty.

On November 22, 1963, I was a junior in high school. Around 1 p.m., our principal's voice came on the loudspeakers. His voice quaked as he announced that the President of the United States, John F. Kennedy, had been killed by an assassin's bullet in Dallas. As we sat limp at our school desks, the principal continued with more detail, most of which we could not absorb. The single fact that the President was dead overloaded our very young circuits. The last thing I heard the principal say was that the basketball game scheduled for that evening had been cancelled.

The rest of the day was all tears and confusion and anger and fear. Rumors quickly spread that the President's death was part of a larger attack on the U.S. Some parents rushed to school to gather up their kids, fearful of some unknown but imminent danger. Students who turned to teachers for strength were just as likely to find teachers as afraid and confused as they were, themselves in need of someone to turn to.

Just before school let out, our principal spoke to us once again over the loudspeakers. He spoke with his familiar strong and in-command voice. He said only that the basketball game previously cancelled would be played that night as scheduled. He urged everyone to attend.

That night, our parents took us to the school early and

dropped us off. Many of them said they wouldn't return to watch us play. A number of parents tried to talk the principal out of playing the game. He stood firm. Most of us didn't feel much like playing basketball. It seemed wrong. In its sadness, the country had come to a halt. No matter how important basketball seemed to us when we had awakened that day, it didn't seem important at all by game time.

It was very quiet down in the locker room. There were no cheers upstairs in the gym. No band playing the school fight song. No sound at all. After years of playing before sold-out crowds, we wondered what it would be like to play with nobody watching. It didn't take long for us to conclude that it really didn't matter. Nothing mattered, really.

We were shocked when we took the floor. The place was packed. Dead quiet, but filled to the rafters. We shot our lay-ups in silence. The buzzer sounded and jolted the crowd, sounding fifty times louder than we remembered it. On the sidelines, we stood for the national anthem. It started hesitantly, low and quiet. But line-by-line, note-by-note, it built. By the time we reached the last two lines, the crowd was singing at the top of its collective lungs, and when the song ended, the spectators sent up a cheer so loud and long it shook the floor.

We played basketball that night, and the spectators lost themselves in the evening, and we began to heal.

Many years later, I visited the principal of my old school, and among the things we talked about was the night the President was killed. I asked him why he had insisted on playing a game the night the nation had lost its leader.

"Because," he said, "I'm an old civics teacher. And for years I taught that America's greatness is not her leaders, but her people and her towns and her schools. When they shot the President, I just wanted to send a message to whoever did it that they killed a man. They didn't kill us."

I've been thinking about my old principal a lot lately. His example guides me. While I will watch with extreme interest the events in the Gulf, I will watch with equal interest the events in our towns and neighborhoods. And I will note with particular sadness the cancellation of any basketball games.

A BASKETBALL FAN'S FUNERAL

Saying farewell to my biggest fan.

Her name was Lacy. There was nothing frilly about her. She once snapped the head off a water moccasin threatening my sister in the garage. Snapped it off just as clean as could be by picking it up by the tail and working the four-foot snake like a bullwhip. She was 4'10" and the toughest woman in the county. She loved basketball and, like her sister Betty, had a deep love-hate relationship with referees. She liked the kind of referees like my Uncle Harry, who would let the players play and not call cheap fouls. She was in the stands at every home game. She gave the referees hell every time they called traveling when the offender did not travel in the least.

She was my mom. And the guy who was often called for traveling was me. In her world, I had never picked up my pivot foot. I never carried the ball, I never double-dribbled, and I never fouled anyone. She let the referees know that they were, among other things, blind, prejudiced against me and any team I played for, on the pad for the opposition, and completely inept.

I often felt sorry for the guys in the striped shirts. If I was called for traveling by the sidelines, near where my mom was sitting, she would jump to her feet (and if spectators in front of her stood up, she would climb up on her seat to be seen and heard), and shout at the top of her lungs something on the order of, "John Henry Miller, that's the third stupid call in the past two minutes. Your mother would be ashamed! Shake your head John Henry, your eyes are stuck!"

One night, toward the end of a close game, I stole the ball at half-court and took it in for a lay-up. One of the guys from the other team beat me to the basket and took a position. The ref called a charge. It was close. It could have gone either way. I was disappointed, but I was okay. Mom wasn't. As I ran down the court to take up my defensive position, I saw Mom climbing over people until she got to the floor and ran the sidelines until she caught up with the referee who had made the call.

"James Oliver Turner, you earned your money tonight. Who paid you to make that stupid call? I'm calling your mother...." Some less ardent fans had her by the arms and shoulders and were pulling her back to her seat.

By my senior year, nobody would sit near my mother, unless it was Aunt Betty. Aunt Betty's lexicon of invectives inspired my mother, and the two of them made the lives of the referees in our gym a sad and lonely experience. Eventually, Aunt Betty's own children grew big enough to play ball at another school, and soon my mom was on her own. Referees would come onto the floor and look for her, and then take up positions away from the bleachers in which she sat. The seven dollars a game they were being paid was simply not enough money to make officiating a game a profitable venture. She continued in this way until I graduated from high school, and then came to no more games.

My mom died at the age of eighty-three. We put on a big funeral for her. We hired a piano player instead of an organist. He played "Peg o' My Heart" and "Tuxedo

Junction" and "Moonlight Serenade." She had loved dancing best, next to basketball. All of her high-heel shoes were set out on a table at the service, and the little girls got to take home a pair of Grandma's dancing shoes. Coach and his wife came to the funeral. Coach always showed up when one of his player's parents died. He showed up even after the boys had grown to men and Coach was bent with arthritis. He had loved Mom. He always considered her part of the team.

At the end of the ceremony, we asked anyone who might have a story about Mom to come to the front of the church and tell it. Several family members talked, and Coach said a word about how much he admired her, and then it was quiet. I looked around to see if anyone was moving and caught the eye of a man just walking into the church. He seemed vaguely familiar to me, but I could not place him. He kept his overcoat on and walked to the pulpit. The church grew quiet as he fiddled with the microphone, and then he said, "My name is Ernie. Lacy knew me as Ernest James Elliot. I was a referee for twenty-five years and I officiated about twenty of her son's games. I always feared going into that gym, and I looked for her in the stands. She gave me the dickens every time I called a foul or an infraction on her kid.

In her eyes, he could never do anything wrong. One time I got fed up with her yelling and criticizing after I had called the boy for traveling, so I called an official time-out, walked up to where she was sitting in the bleachers, and took off my whistle and offered it her, and said, 'Lacy, if you can do a better job of this than I'm doing, then put on a striped shirt and take this whistle and get into the game.' Well, she didn't take it, and for the rest of the game, we didn't hear a peep from her. For all the trouble she gave me, she taught me something meaningful. She taught me how much she loved that boy."

Then the old man stepped down from the pulpit and walked to Mom's urn on the table. He reached inside his overcoat collar and pulled out the lanyard and whistle around his neck and put it on the table with all her treasured mementos. And I heard him say, "Call a fair game, Lacy."

SHAKE IT OFF

Sometimes the lessons are painful.

"Shake it off," I said. My twelve-year-old had stumbled during a full-court dribbling exercise. She sat on the floor, holding her knee.

The other father-coaches walked quickly to her and helped her to stand. I could see she wasn't hurt too badly. No tears. But she had a limp. It was a good limp. It had the other father-coaches convinced she had really hurt herself. I was her father, and I knew better. When she stumbled in front of everyone, she was embarrassed. I knew how that felt. I might have even faked an injury in a situation like that. Nobody likes to be made fun of, and faking an injury can shut people up pretty fast. I knew that. I knew she knew that.

So that's why I took my time walking over to her. I wanted her to know that I knew she wasn't hurt.

"Shake it off," I said again. Then I bent close to her ear and said, "I'll help you up and we can go out in the hallway. After you get over your embarrassment, you can get back into the practice."

"I really did hurt my knee, Dad, I promise," she said.

"Fine," I said. "Let's just shake it off, whaddya say?" She put on a bigger show of getting off the court, I thought, than when she had tried to get up. Now I was sort of embarrassed. I could sense the other coaches knew Ashley was faking. I thought I saw that knowledgeable look in their eyes. I looked back into those eyes and sheepishly grinned and nodded. The expression said, 'You know how it is. I'll calm her down and she'll be back in a minute.'

"Shake it off," I said in the hallway. She said she was trying to. She was starting to sob. It's a confusing age, I thought.

"I'm sorry, Dad. It did hurt, though."

"I'm sure it did. Just don't put on a show. Just shake it off and get back in the practice." I thought I sounded wonderfully father- and coach-like. And she did get back in the practice. She went right back out there and tried to run a weaving exercise with the rest of the girls. But there was still a hint of a limp. Couldn't let it go completely, I thought.

"Ashley, if you're going to limp, we might as well take you home," I said. I knew that would get her to stop pretending.

"No, Dad, I can play. Watch." She grabbed a ball and dribbled it across the gym. The limp was hardly noticeable.

"That a girl!" I said. That's how she'd been taught. Tough it out. Hang in there. Shake it off.

After practice we had a long talk about how the great competitors play with pain. She sensed that I was disappointed with the way she had put on a display right after the stumble. I'm certain she was ashamed of herself for embarrassing me.

The next morning she was off to school as usual and I was off to work. I didn't see her again until that evening when I came home for dinner. "How's the knee?" I asked.

"Fine, I guess," she answered.

I knew it would be. I was smug. I had been a good father-coach. I had seen through the whole thing and I had taught a good and lasting lesson.

The following day Ashley limped down to the breakfast table.

"My knee, Dad. It hurts bad." I glanced over the newspaper and looked down at her leg. The knee was swollen the size of a cantaloupe. I closed my eyes. I took a deep breath. I called the orthopedist. Within an hour she was being examined. The x-ray showed the kneecap was blown out. The muscles holding it in place were ripped, shredded. Arthroscopic surgery was recommended. Immediately.

I began apologizing to her as we drove to the hospital. I had no excuse, I told her. I was just so very, very sorry that I hadn't responded to her as a father, but as a father-coach. She said she understood.

I continued to apologize to her as she was being prepared for surgery. I told her that I thought she was faking because that is probably what I would have done in the same situation. I told her it was wrong for me to think she would react the same way. She said it was okay. I told her that I loved her and that I should never have doubted her pain. I told her I had learned a very important lesson, and that I would always be sorry for how I had behaved.

"Shake it off," she said. "Just shake it off, Dad."

"I can't, Ashley," I said. "Not yet."

CERTIFICATES

Sometimes milestones are made of paper.

Summer basketball camp had been a terrific experience, right up until the very end. That's when they handed out the awards. There were trophies for the best shooter, best dribbler, best defense, best team, most improved, and so on. It seemed like everyone got some kind of trophy. The rest of us got participation certificates. I hate participation certificates. To most people these are simply documents attesting to the fact that you showed up somewhere. To me they have always been decrees of failure. I didn't even want to bring this one home. I had hoped I would be able to show off to my dad a nice "best shooter" trophy or something. No such luck.

So when I walked up the driveway, I began to make up excuses for why I was coming home virtually empty-handed. I was ashamed of myself for not being better than I was. I was afraid I was becoming a disappointment to my parents. I figured they had just about had it with my certificates of participation. I knew Mom would say, "That's a very nice certificate. I think we have a frame around here somewhere." But I knew she would really be thinking, "I guess this is about your fiftieth certificate of participation, isn't it? When does all this money we're spending on camps result in, say, a trophy, for instance?"

That's why I tried to sneak into the house, but Dad saw me first. "How was camp?" he asked.

"I didn't win any trophies because I was on a stupid team," I shouted. "But I won this certificate."

"How?" Dad asked.

"How? By showing up with my gym bag, that's how."

"That's good," said Dad. "That's real good."

I knew he hated me. I knew he wished he had had a different son. I went to my room and threw the certificate into a box with all the rest and shoved the box way to the back of the closet. Meaningless things, I thought. Who needs basketball, anyway?

I was sitting at my bedroom window, looking out on the basketball goal at the edge of the driveway, when Dad walked in and sat down on the bed.

"You know," he began, "I never got any of these certificate things. Wish I had, though."

"Why?" I asked. "They're just paper, nothing special."

"Because they represent how hard you've tried. I don't have any way of telling how much effort I put into being better. You've got all these certificates. You must be proud. I am."

"But I wasn't the best at anything, Dad," I said.

"You aren't supposed to be the best right now," he said.

"Then, what am I supposed to be?" I asked.

"Patient," he said, closing the door as he left.

THE COMPETITION

Be careful what you wish for.

T wo weeks before practice was to start, E.J. Fields moved in across the street. He was my age and my height and first came into my sight spinning a Wilson Last Bilt on his knuckle. He arrived with a brand new ball and a reputation. E.J. had played ball in town. His father's decision to move to the country was not a good choice, in my book. The boy wasn't the greatest basketball player in the world, but he was better than me, and that was an unusually disturbing quality at this particular time. Just one day before E.J. moved in, I had held a virtual lock on the only open starting guard position on the high school team, an all-conference senior holding the other.

I didn't exactly roll out the welcome wagon. As a matter of fact, I couldn't stop thinking of ways to get E.J.'s father transferred back to the city, or India. I used my study halls to draw stick pictures of E.J. suffering unspeakable humiliations. I dreamed of debilitating viruses finding their way into E.J.'s Jell-O salad. I made up and spread stories that E.J. had done serious jail time. But nothing worked. E.J. was still better than me.

On the first day of practice, the coach broke the team into two units. The guys who had started or were expected to start got the new red jerseys; the second five got the old whites. I got a red and E.J. got a white. This, of course, was as it should be. I had played with some of these guys since the second grade. We had developed, some people said, a sort of telepathic basketball communication. As a unit, the five of us hummed like a well-oiled watch. It would take E.J. five years to get to know these ballplayers the way I did.

Three days later, the coach told me to give E.J. my red jersey.

For the next two weeks my best subject was sulking. Life had turned unfair and unpleasant. I now used my study halls to examine everything I had ever done in my life that might have angered the Almighty and moved Him to punish me with E.J. I could not understand what I had done to deserve

E.J. moving to my school. At practice, my play was less than inspired. I began to lose interest in the game. That attitude eventually became so obvious that the coach called me into the cage for one of his talks.

"Son, are you upset that E.J.'s starting and you're not?" he asked.

"No," I said.

He said that was good, because he would be real angry if I was going to "act that selfishly." He went on to tell me how the team was more important than the individual, and I claimed that I understood that. He said compared to making a contribution to the team, starting was not important. I began to feel ashamed of myself for wanting to start. I sat there trying to be a better person, but I couldn't. Coach talked to me for an hour, and by the end I still wanted that red jersey. He said E.J. would start as long as he continued playing the way he was and I continued playing the way I was.

My basketball dreams began to shift. For years I had visualized myself orchestrating win upon varsity win from the tip-off. Now I was more likely to imagine E.J. starting, but humiliating himself with blunder upon delicious blunder. The crowd would begin to chant my name, beseeching the coach to go to his secret weapon: me, "The Sixth Man." I began to grow uncomfortably comfortable with the job title.

But before the first game of the season, I got the red jersey back and was named a starter. I wish I could say I earned it, but I didn't. E.J. developed a bulge on his knee. The doctor said it was Osgood Slaughter Disease. They said he grew too fast and now had to have his whole leg in a cast for almost a year. I was, undoubtedly, responsible. I had openly hoped for something like this. One of the pictures I had drawn in study hall was a stick man with a cast on his stick leg.

The next year, E.J. moved to another state. He eventually got his cast off, played ball, and went on to college. Over the years, I've become almost certain that I didn't cause E.J.'s leg problem. I have nearly convinced myself that any connection between E.J.'s knee and my selfishness is very probably not much more than coincidence. However, it's been a long time since I have drawn a stick figure that was anything but perfectly healthy.

EYEBROW SHAVE

The art of doing one thing very well.

The short, roundish figure of O.D. (Odie) Barnett appeared at the end of my driveway and dread crept up the back of my neck. I turned away from him, hoping he'd disappear. Odie was a basketball menace. He had been cut from every team for which he'd ever tried out. But he was a gifted shot. Not in the conventional way. Odie had no jump shot, but he could stand with his back to the hoop and throw down basket after basket from twenty feet. He practiced for hours shots that were unlawful in a regulation game. He knew the slant of everyone's garage roof. He could fire up long-distance shots that bounced off the roof and into the hoop. He could drop-kick baskets from half-court. He could bounce them in off the pavement and off the top of his head. He was a trick shot artist, and the game of H.O.R.S.E. was his stock and trade.

Odie strode up the driveway with his old MacGregor leather ball under his arm. I had never beaten Odie in a game of H.O.R.S.E., and it was senseless to bet against him. But Odie wouldn't play unless there was "a little something" on the game. And pride and honor demanded a varsity ballplayer always accept an Odie challenge. The bet was never money, because none of us had any. Odie could dream up the most distasteful punishment for losing to him—for that is what it was, punishment. One month it was the "buck naked lap." Upon the conclusion of the game, the loser was honor-bound to take off every stitch of clothing and run around the house one time. That form of wager lasted until a neighbor lady complained. Our parents counseled us and introduced us to the term "morals charge." They told us that being caught naked in your yard by the police would result in a mark on your record that would never go away. They said it would prevent us from becoming bank presidents and preachers, and that no one would understand that the charge resulted from a missed left-handed hook shot from the open bedroom window.

And so it was that Odie appeared in my driveway looking for a new game and a new punishment for me in the form of a wager. He walked over to the milk box and placed atop its lid a brand new Gillette safety razor. Then he turned and smiled at me and said, "Horse?"

"What's the razor for, Odie?"

"For your eyebrow," said Odie. "You lose, you shave off your eyebrow."

"Shoot for first shot," I said. My only hope was that I'd get first shot and keep him on the defensive. Odie picked up the ball, walked to the lawn, and swung up a looping hook shot. *Swish.*

"I start," he said.

He chose for his first shot a no-look prayer.

"Left, off the glass, from behind the car." He could not see the basket from where he was standing. "Ka-chunk!" he shouted in unison with the sound made by the ball hitting the backboard and pocketing in the net.

My shot was wide by ten feet. "H," he said. The next two shots were identical. Odie hiked the ball between his legs from mid-court. Both of my shots went over the garage. His fourth shot came from the side of the garage.

"Over the corner, over the telephone wire," he shouted from out of sight. Then the ball appeared as it sailed over the electrical line, over the gable of the roof, and into the center of the basket. My shot got tangled in the telephone wire and fell feebly back into my hands. "I believe you now have S," said Odie. I wondered what it would be like to not have eyebrows.

Odie disappeared into the screened porch. "Watch carefully," he said. The screen door flew open and Odie careened down the steps, the ball in hand. At the point between two towering spruce trees, he heaved up a shot that came down short, slamming into the pavement.

"Missed!" I yelled.

"Not yet," yelled Odie.

The ball hit the pavement and rebounded high into the air. It came down softly against the backboard before settling into the hoop.

"Your shot," he said.

Absently, I walked onto the porch while pinching my eyebrow, perhaps for the last time. I ran off the porch and pushed up a shot between the two trees. I shouldn't have wasted my time.

"That would be the game," said Odie, as he handed me the Gillette. I chose the right eyebrow. It took only two passes to shave it clean. Odie took the razor back from my limp hand. "I'll be needing that," he said.

I watched Odie leave, headed for another home court he'd memorized. That year Odie took seventeen eyebrows before the parents put an end to the practice. I remember it was a Sunday afternoon when we were told there would be no more "eyebrow shaves." I remember feeling a deep sense of relief, until Monday afternoon, when I saw Odie walk up the driveway with a can of dog food and a spoon.

CONSTANT COMPANION

"The basketball should be a part of you."

"Show me the ball," he yelled. "You'd darn well better have that ball with you, son." It was the coach. I sat in my dad's Plymouth at the light. Coach had pulled up next to me and was now glaring impatiently. "Show me the ball," he growled.

I knew I shouldn't have come this way. I knew this was the coach's regular route. I knew basketball season was coming. I knew I shouldn't have Jeannie Simms in the car with me. I knew I had better be able to find a basketball in this car somewhere—and now.

"Coach, it was here this morning, 'cause me and Charlie Hixon practiced give-and-go's for about a hundred hours and…who? Oh, Jeannie Simms. And I know Charlie put it back…pardon? Oh, a cheerleader from the city. We were talking about the season and stuff."

"The rock, son. Show me the rock," said the coach. I took my arm from around Jeannie Simms and began using it to shovel through about a thousand pounds of fast food debris on the floor of the back seat. "It was here this morning, Coach. I swear to God." The light changed. Was it my imagination or had it suddenly turned much colder than it had been all summer?

As I eased the big Plymouth through the intersection, I thought back to the last day of class three months ago, when the coach had handed out those brand new balls to all the returning lettermen. It was one of his traditions. Made me feel proud. He warned us, "I don't want to catch you anywhere, at any time, without this basketball at your side, boys." And then the coach said he didn't want any 'lollygaggin'.' When Coach talked about "lollygaggin," he was talking about girls. Coach didn't like girls, much.

He said girls and basketball didn't mix well. He said girls distracted a ballplayer and that there would be enough time for 'lollygaggin' ' when we were too old to play basketball. He said 'lollygaggin' ' sapped a ballplayer's energy on game day. All of us knew what he was talking about, but none of us thought *he* did.

He'd given us those basketballs because he wanted us to use them—to cherish them. They were brand new Wilson Last Bilts and they were leather and he didn't care if we used them outdoors and wore all the little bumps of grain right off of them, as long as we "for-Criminy-sakes-used- 'em." I looked over to the coach and he jerked his head to the right in a move I had seen state troopers make. It meant: *pull over*.

I swung the Plymouth into a closed-for-the-season root beer stand. I felt sick. Here I sat with Jeannie Simms at my side instead of a basketball. I was ashamed. Coach thought I'd been 'lollygaggin',' and I hadn't. But I'd never convince him.

"Thought you wanted that other starting guard position this year, son."

"I do, Coach. Man, of course I do," I shot back through the window. Where was that daggone basketball?

"Just show me the ball. I trusted you with it. I just want to know that you have kept it with you this summer."

A lie began to build in the back of my throat and started out of my mouth. I stopped it. I couldn't lie to the coach. I could lie to the history teacher, or the principal, for that matter. But not to the coach.

"I don't have it with me, Coach. I always do. It's been here every day, but I don't have it right now for some reason."

"I'm real disappointed in you, Shelb'. I thought that starting spot was something you really wanted. Guess I was wrong." He put his car in gear and rolled up the window. I sat there feeling like I was all head, like I didn't have any arms or legs—no feeling, except a dullness in my ears and the sense that my throat was swelling up. Then Coach rolled down the window and looked at me sadly and said, "Tell your mom and dad I said hello." Then he drove off.

"You can take me home if you want," Jeannie said softly.

"Sure," I said. "I'm not feeling too hot."

I took Jeannie to her house by the city school and drove myself home. When I pulled up to the house, Mom was standing there, holding the basketball on her hip. "Coach called," she hollered. "Said you'd probably be coming home for this. Said he found you driving around with Jeannie without your basketball."

"I know," I said.

"I told him it was your dad's fault," she said.

"What?"

"I told him that your dad had taken the ball out to shoot around this morning and hadn't put it back."

My heart jumped. My mom had lied to the coach to save my career. I couldn't believe it. I had heard that mothers would often do heroic things for their young, like rip the doors off burning cars and stuff. But this? She told a lie to a coach. I felt mixed up.

"Mom, you didn't have to lie."

"I didn't," she said. "Your father was irresponsible and didn't put it back after he borrowed it."

That's right. I *had* seen the old man this morning firing up odd-looking set shots. But that didn't matter now. I was saved. My mom had saved my life, just as sure as if she'd tore off a car door.

"Did he say anything else, Mom?"

"No," she said. "Only that practice starts October 15th."

RUNNING UP THE SCORE

Play with honor.

My mother would have washed my mouth out with soap had she heard me. I had called a man a name at a basketball game. A bad name. In fact, I called him this bad name in front of the parents of the children he was coaching. I called him this bad name in front of the parents of children I was coaching. It was a very bad name, and I want to take this opportunity to say publicly that I'm glad I did it.

The coach in question fielded a strong team of seventh graders against my proud bunch. Shortly after tip-off, the score was 23-0. It was the full-court press. Despite my coaching acumen and the team's pride, we crossed the ten-second line only three times in the first half, and on each of those occasions the guards made snappy bounce passes to someone on the other team.

My blood began to percolate as the half drew to a close. My frustrated and humiliated players were trapped in the relentless press, and despite the 23-0 score, the coach wouldn't call it off. My players shot looks of despair to the bench, as if asking me to do something, anything, to end this suffering. I was going to call time-out, but we couldn't keep the ball long enough.

When the half ended, I brought the team to the corner of the gym and drew up an emergency offense. I didn't bother to diagram a play to break the press, because, I told them, the other team wouldn't come out in the second half in the press. I said that based on years of basketball play. Years of fair play. Years of faith that the human being was basically a gentle animal. Years of knowledge that grown men do not needlessly inflict pain on children.

My years had taught me nothing.

The coach installed the press against my team as soon as his team scored the first basket. This was roughly the point at which the bad word came out of my mouth, the first time. Upon hurling the word at the opposing coach, the noise went out of the gym like so much air from a punctured ball. Mothers behind the other team's bench looked shocked and mortified. Mothers from behind my bench joined me in the saying of the word. The fan support was meaningful and gave me strength.

I told one of my players on the court to call time-out if we ever got the ball again, and within minutes they were gathered around me, awaiting my genius. They were disappointed that I didn't have any innovative basketball plays to diagram. I only told them what I knew. I said that the coach of the other team did not understand the game of basketball. I apologized to them on behalf of all adults who fail to take into account the hearts of children. I told them that real competitors do not relish or find joy in the act of humiliating the opponent. I said that it was a long-held notion among honorable coaches that running up the score against an outmatched team was the work of classless men with something to prove. I told them I had no answers. I told them to try to have fun in the game that remained. I told them I was sorry.

The girls scored twenty-one straight points. Not enough to win, but enough to be proud. As we left the gym, I began thinking about the bad word. I knew I should have my mouth washed out with soap. I also knew that no amount of soap could get out the bad taste in my mouth left by a coach with too much to prove.

ROAD TRIP
BASKETBALL

Make it a game anytime, anywhere.

Barbara, the three girls, and I drove through southeastern Minnesota one October. We were there to enjoy the change of seasons, to ride bicycles, and to visit several small communities. When we set out on our trip, I had no inkling that the road we traveled would take me on a basketball journey.

After visiting Lanesboro, Whalan, Peterson, and Rushford, we headed to Wabasha. The Hall Family ran the Anderson House there, and we visited them every time we were near the river town. Three years earlier, on one of those visits, my oldest daughter, Ashley, struck up a very serious basketball rivalry with the Hall's oldest son, John. Ashley had won the first meeting, and John spent the next year, his father says, practicing into the wee hours, vowing never to let that happen again.

The second meeting bore the fruit of his practice, and he emerged the victor and won the bragging rights, which he exercised at every opportunity. The rivalry, from its first moments, has been spiced with letters and face-to-face challenges. There had been a lot of chin music in this rivalry; Ashley and John had carried on those past two years like Larry Bird and Magic Johnson. Each day, both of these people spent a little time thinking about putting it in the other's face. It was my kind of relationship.

As we pulled into Wabasha and began winding our way through the historic streets toward the Anderson House Hotel, we saw in the distance a game. Five guys were playing breakneck basketball on the concrete of an old gasoline station. Two on three. Two big guys against three little guys. One of the younger players was John Hall.

I was seized by impulse. I drove the car directly at the gasoline station, screeched to a halt, and shouted, "John

Hall, you ain't nothin'. We've come for a rematch. We will take all of you."

Barbara and the girls stared wide-eyed at one another. I threw open the door and shot a cocky sneer at the boys. The people in my car sat very still, trying to disappear from view. "Come on," I said. "We can wax these guys."

My wife and the three girls slowly got out of the car. The boys looked at one another, then began matching up. A guy about 6'1" said, "I got her." He was pointing to Barbara. She is five feet tall. In fact, everyone on my team, except me, was under 5'3".

John, of course, immediately matched up with Ashley, and they began a rancorous hoop dialogue having to do with what one would do to the other's backside. My middle daughter Lacy guarded a guy who wore a big blue metal knee brace and said he'd ruptured his anterior cruciate ligament. I told her to tell him that she suffered from a character defect and was known to play dirty from time to time. She told him that she might, without thinking, step on the back of his knee. The guy was neutralized from the start of the game.

The youngest daughter, Delta, matched up with Bobby the Blur. Bobby is thirteen and thinks he's Michael Jordan. After five minutes of guarding him, Delta agreed. I took the big guy, a 6'6" junior. I told him I had a heart condition.

My wife played what might charitably be described as outfield. The game was tough. I hadn't expected the boys to play as hard as they did. I thought they'd say, "Oh, they're just girls." But apparently John had spread around Ashley's brash challenges, so the boys played for keeps. They went up on us quickly. It didn't help that Barbara kept making what she called "friendly passes," which the boys kept stealing. It didn't help that The Blur hit everything he threw up. It didn't help that John had perfected a three-point shot from the out-of-bounds line.

Two guys happened along and wanted to play. Lacy and Barbara came out of the game. No more "friendly passes." Ashley tightened her defense against John, and the score evened up. Ashley drove twice and the guy dropped off me and rejected her shot. Seriously rejected. The ball ended up in the hedge next door. The boys laughed. Bad thing to do. Ashley set her jaw and took the ball inside hard the next time. She jabbed left and went right, spun, head-faked and sent the whole frontline into the sky. Just as they began their helpless descent, she kissed the glass with an underhand right. Bobby shouted, "Goodnight!" and high fives were exchanged boy to girl.

It went on like that for an hour. Back and forth, highlight and lowlight. I sweat through my good clothes, and all of us wore on our faces the grit from the gas station's court. By the end, nobody knew the score. It had been a proper game.

We adjourned to the historic Anderson House for a round of Grandma's chicken and dumplings. After dessert, we said our goodbyes to the Halls. Ashley and John exchanged good-natured challenges about next year. They parted with a high five. Well satisfied, we drove the river road back to the Twin Cities. Inside the car we retold the highlights and we laughed at Mom's friendly passes. We smelled of sweat and good times. We reeked of basketball.

SCHOOL SHOES

Get them any way you can.

Before LeBron James and Kobe, before Nike and Adidas, before the advent of the hundred-dollar sneakers, there were Chuck Taylor Converse All-Stars. It was the greatest basketball shoe of its time. Nobody knew who Chuck Taylor was, and it didn't matter. If you wore a Converse All-Star, you were recognized as an official ballplayer.

Expensive for their time, the shoes cost about fifteen dollars. Keds and Red Ball Jets were much cheaper, but no self-respecting basketball player would ever be caught in such a shoe. No, the Converse All-Star was the item, and youngsters in my town longed for a pair.

You could whine about your Keds and try to make your mother ashamed for making you wear such humiliating footwear. You could wait for Christmas and hope Santa would spring for some new Chuck Taylors. Or you could be awarded your own All-Stars by the high school coach. My school issued these prized shoes to each person who'd survived the final cut and made varsity. We called them "school shoes," and the term carried momentous weight. "Where'd you get your Chuck Taylors?" they'd ask. "School shoes," you'd answer. "Golly," was the usual response.

In my freshman year, I tried for some Converse All-Stars by covering all bases. I whined about my Keds to my mother, I asked for a pair for Christmas, and I tried out for varsity. There was about as much chance of me making the varsity as my whining inspiring my mother to buy me a pair.

So I was left to pray that I would find a pair of All-Stars under the tree come Christmas. But that, too, was a long shot. You see, at my house, a guy only got new shoes when the ones he was currently wearing grew so small on his feet that his toenails cut through the canvas. Even when the glue holding the rubber to the canvas came undone and flapped when you ran, that wasn't enough for my mom. As long as there was a roll of tape or rubber cement somewhere in the house, she believed "you can get a couple more months out of the ones you have."

In other words, I had no hope.

On the third day of December, we all went to the cage to look at the bulletin board. There, Coach had posted the names of players who had survived the last cut. Here were the people who would be wearing school shoes. These were people who didn't have to whine or wait until Christmas. I was not one of them.

I spent the first two weeks of December playing on the freshman team and suffering the humiliation of wearing my taped-together Keds and flopping up and down the court. I was a failure, my life had no meaning, and I had no reasonable expectation that things would improve. But then again, I hadn't given mononucleosis any consideration.

The illness swept through the varsity. It knocked three guys out for the season. Since it was called the kissing disease, the big talk was about where they got it. All I could think about was who would take their place on the team.

On the Friday before Christmas vacation, Coach walked into study hall and asked the teacher, "Is Shelby in here?"

"Yes," she replied, and pointed to me in the back of the room. "Here, Coach," I shouted.

"Check in at the cage after school, Shelb," he said. I said that I would, and the coach started to leave. Then he turned and said, "What size shoe do you wear?"

"Ten," I shouted.

I sat staring at the door for a full minute after the coach had closed it behind him. My neighbor leaned over and whispered, "School shoes?"

"Chuck Taylor Converse All-Stars."

"Golly."

OLD TIMERS' GAME

If you were once a ballplayer, it will ever be thus.

I hadn't seen these guys in more than twenty-five years. A quarter of a century ago we had gone thirty-six straight games without a loss. A lot of folks who packed the gymnasium this night remembered us as the best team to have ever played for the school. That's why they selected us to come back and play in the first annual Old Timers' Game.

The announcer introduced the players one by one. "At six-seven, at center, number fifty-two...Tommy Evans!" The guy who limped out to center court didn't look like the Tommy Evans I had known. He looked like Tommy's old man.

"At forward, six-foot-six, number thirty-three…Willie Crabtree!" Wicked Willie Crabtree could dunk two-handed in the sixth grade. It was apparent, as Willie waddled onto the court, that the only thing he'd been dunking recently was glazed doughnuts.

"At the other forward, standing six-feet-eight-inches, number thirty-five…Eugene Clevenger." Gene the Bean. He'd been a skinny kid with fluid, gliding moves and a jump shot that sent the ball floating to the hoop like a feather. Tonight he looked like the preacher he'd become, except fatter.

"At guard, six-foot-two-inches, number ten, Darnell Aiken." Darnell had been the state 100-yard dash champion. There was early talk of the Olympics and pro football. Neither panned out. Twenty-five years ago, Darnell was the finest physical specimen in the state. Tonight he looked like he had not aged a day.

The announcer introduced me as "Number twelve in your program but number one in his own mind…"

Then a middle-aged woman wearing a cheerleader's outfit walked out to accept a bouquet of roses.

"Know who that is?" Tommy Evans asked.

"Barbara Bush," I replied.

"No," said Tommy. "That's Linda Campbell." She had been head cheerleader in the class behind us.

"Geez, she looks old," I said.

"She's my wife," said Tommy, looking even more like his old man.

We were pitted against a reunion team from a school across town. It looked like a reunion of retired chemistry teachers to me, but Willie said he'd heard they had been practicing for six months.

One minute and fifteen seconds into the game, Tommy Evans called time-out and asked someone to take his pulse. One of our subs was a veterinarian. He held Tommy's wrist and said it might be serious. The vet looked at me and smiled that same stupid high school smile he used to give me when he was lying and the only person who knew it was me. Doc just wanted in the game. A minute later, Tommy was on the bench thinking about his wife and kids.

The first half ended with a tie score, a broken finger, a dozen blisters, and the promise of sundry aches and pains tomorrow. Most of the second half was plodding. We traded baskets and played little or no defense. But with under two minutes left to play, something happened. The band struck up the school fight song. I hadn't heard that song in years. I could see in the guys' eyes that the song was affecting them as it was me. It was like a shot of youth elixir. Time began to spin in reverse. I crossed the ten-second line and it was like crossing into the Twilight Zone. For starters, Willie Crabtree shot out to the wing. He didn't walk out, he shot out.

Without thinking, I ran a low pick and rolled off. Willie's pass was perfect. As I continued into the lane to shoot, the weak-side defensive forward slipped across the lane to close me out. Instinctively, I dropped a blind pass behind my back. It happened automatically, the way it had so many times long ago. Simultaneous with the pick-and-roll, Darnell had taken off from the point, slashing through the middle. The drop pass landed in his waiting hands and his dunk shook the gym and its inhabitants.

We played like that until the horn sounded. Two minutes of basketball and a free trip back to 1965. For two minutes we were as good as we ever were, and each of us thought for a brief moment, "We can do this." For a moment we tried to make our imaginations concoct a life in which we were no longer grown-ups with families, no longer adults with jobs. Just basketball players.

After the game, Tommy Evans was reassured by a physician that he wasn't going to die. That made him happy and he left to go home to his reality with the head cheerleader, the mother of his children. My reality paid a visit at the coffee shop around the corner from the school.

"Mr. Shelby?" the waitress said.

"Yes?"

"Did you go to the game tonight?" she asked.

"Yes," I said brightly.

"How did your son play?" she inquired. "I went to school with Don. Would you tell him Darla says hi?"

"I'll tell him, Darla," I said. I finished my coffee and limped into the sunset.

CAUGHT IN THE ACT

No matter how old we are, we still play the game in our hearts.

There's a whole bunch of people my age who look upon today's ballplayer with awe. For those of us to whom the simple act of touching the rim was a cause for celebration, the aerial acrobatics of today's long-legged leapers is hard to comprehend. The thrill of jumping so high that you can look down into the basket has always eluded us. We will never take off from the foul line, tuck the ball in the crook of our arms, and glide toward the basket for fifteen or twenty seconds before driving the ball deep into the cylinder. We will never do that. It is out of our reach.

Or is it?

The publisher of a local newspaper one day offered to sell me the latest in contrivances designed to boost the sagging egos of has-been ballplayers: the adjustable goal. He told me that the rim and backboard could be lowered to eight feet. He pitched the device as a great teaching tool for younger players. He said it would be perfect for developing a small player's shooting eye. He said that a guy might even try dunking on it. Being interested in the shooting eyes of young players, I immediately bought the contraption and had it installed on my driveway court.

The next day I invited all the kids in the neighborhood to come over and develop their shooting eyes. They had a wonderful time. They kept asking me to dunk the ball. I told them the goal was there to help them, not me. They said I looked like Yao Ming standing next to the eight-foot basket. I thought they'd never go home.

That night, after everyone had gone to bed, I quietly slipped out into the garage, where, earlier in the day, I had stashed the authentic Chicago Bulls uniform and the family's video camera. I quietly slipped into the Bulls jersey and suitably baggy pants. I set the camera on the tripod and aimed it at the eight-foot goal. I dragged an extension cord out onto the court and plugged in an industrial work light. And then, when all was ready, I took from its box a Spalding Junior Size basketball. It was no bigger than a cantaloupe, and it fit into my hand like a normal ball fits into Shaq's.

I focused the camera, pressed the button, and ran into the glow of the lights. My first dunk was unspectacular. I was taking the measure of my capacity to jam. My second was fiercer. The next had special character, and I had my tongue sticking out the whole time. I then began a series of off-the-glass rebound slamma-jammas. The goal shook on its post. The vibration only made me want more.

My next feat was a feeble attempt at a 360-degree Gorilla. I only got about 223 degrees around, and slammed the ball into the underside of the rim. I took a five-minute break to erase the last attempt from the tape. When I resumed the dunk-o-rama, I was a virtual one-man highlight reel. I demonstrated for the camera a no-look jam. I nearly ripped off the backboard with a Hatchet Slam. I split the night air with the racket from my Sky Walker Rocket Jam. I exhausted myself with countless other variations of one- and two-handed reverse in-your-face expressions of the dunkmaster's art.

But I was saving the best for last. The Michael Jordan foul-line takeoff Airborne Tomahawk. I walked to the end of the court, announcing to the camera as I went, "Don Shelby will now attempt to snatch the NBA all-time dunking crown from the head of Michael Jordan. The crowd is holding its collective breath as Shelby prepares the dunk of a lifetime."

I took a deep breath, ran the length of the court, sliced into the glow of the lights, took off from a piece of tape I pretended was the foul line, and rose through the air, where my hang time was so serious that I passed through several time zones. And then I jammed the ball through the hoop with an attitude that would make LeBron James look like a shrinking violet. "Yes!" I shouted, and fell to the asphalt, spent.

At first I thought the polite applause was part of my dream world. But in my dream world I wouldn't have recognized the giggling voices of my next-door neighbors, Herb and Edna.

"How long have you been there?" I asked without getting up.

"A while," Herb said, laughing. "Mosquitoes are terrible."

"I would like to ask a personal favor," I began.

"Don't worry," Herb interjected. "We won't tell a soul."

"Thanks," I said with relief.

"But," Herb said, "We were wondering if we could get a copy of that tape."

"No problem," I said, staring up into the night sky.

A couple minutes passed, and then Edna spoke the words that would allow me to stand and walk away unashamed. She said, "Don, is that goal regulation height?"

"Yes," I said, as I walked back to the house. "Yes, Edna, it is. And you can pick up that videotape in the morning."

THE WIZARD

Know the grace of greatness.

I t will happen in every young basketball player's home. The child looks at the parent and asks, "Who was the best you ever saw play?" One day, when I was a kid, I asked my mom. She was washing dishes and I was sitting at the kitchen table. She didn't turn around, didn't even hesitate, her voice bouncing off the window like a bank-shot.

"When I was in high school at Muncie Central, we went to the state finals a couple of times, and won it all once. But, back in '27, we played Martinsville in the final game. They beat us—or I should say, he beat us."

"Who?" I asked.

"The Rubber Man."

"Who?"

"His name was Johnny Wooden. He was the quickest thing I'd ever seen. I had never seen anyone, then or since, play like he played. Beat us single-handedly. He went on to Purdue, I think, and got involved in professional basketball, but after that I lost track of him. But I can't help but think of him from time to time. I've often wondered what became of Johnny Wooden."

Her question would be answered by my senior year. In 1965, Coach John Wooden led his UCLA Bruins to the first of his record-setting ten national championships. That same year, he wrote the first of his many books on basketball. I bought one and gave it to my mother. I wrote inside the front flap, "Now you know."

One of the magical things about my life is that, many years later, I got a chance to know Coach Wooden. The first time I met him was in Minneapolis, at the celebration of the fiftieth anniversary of the NCAA basketball tournament. Why Minneapolis? Because that city was the site of the very first intercollegiate basketball game ever played. It pitted Hamline University against the Minnesota School of Agriculture in 1895. So, the NCAA put on a dinner to commemorate the anniversary of the big tournament (which, in the beginning, played second banana to the "real" college basketball tournament—the NIT). I was asked to serve as the host of the evening's speeches and to introduce the legendary coach.

At the head table, on either side of me, were Coach John Wooden and the great George Mikan. There it was on the program. How I wished my mother were alive to see it. My name listed with the greatest names in basketball. I'm sure she would have reminded me that I was just the master of ceremonies.

During the meal, I said to Coach Wooden that I would introduce him in a way he had never been introduced before. He smiled his beneficent smile and said, "Son, I don't think that can be done."

When it was time for me to start the program, I began the introduction as thousands had and went on to introduce the greatest basketball coach in NCAA history. I listed his accomplishments. I talked of his ten national titles, of his players who went on to professional stardom, of his incredible success, and his books.

But then I started talking about him as a player. It was not something he was used to. Few people knew that Coach Wooden was only one of two people to be inducted into basketball's Hall of Fame as a coach and as a player. I worked backward from his professional playing career to his storied performances in the Big Ten, and then I went back to Martinsville, Indiana, in 1927.

The final score was 26-23, and Johnny Wooden was called the Rubber Man because of the way he bounced all over the floor and seemed to stretch himself so that he was always in two places at once. I looked down and saw Coach Wooden was staring at his unfinished dinner. He didn't like people talking about the greatness of his playing career. He was much more comfortable putting young players into the spotlight, and I started to get the feeling that I was embarrassing him.

So I wrapped up by saying that Coach Wooden was not only the best coach in the history of college basketball, "But he was also the finest basketball player my mother, Lacy Shelby, ever saw play the game."

The crowd rose to its feet for the coach, and the applause was loud and sustained. He stood quietly and accepted the ovation as only a humble man would. When everyone took their seats, the generous coach told the crowd that I had said I would introduce him as he'd never been introduced before, and that he had doubted that.

"I shouldn't have doubted him," he said, looking at me. "That was the best introduction I have ever had. And Don, I wish your mother were here tonight to see this. She would be proud of you." Coach wiped away a tear. I dabbed my eyes at more than a few. And then the coach began his speech, talking not about college basketball, as he usually did, but about high school ball.

"You know, they have a thing in that state called the Indiana High School All-Time Starting Five. I was honored to be named one of the two starting guards on that team. The other is Oscar Robertson.

"Recently, I was back in Indiana for the NCAA finals, and I was picked up at the airport by an old friend, who knew about basketball, and that all-time first team. I got in the passenger seat and he started driving toward my hotel in Indianapolis. About halfway there he said, 'Coach, have you ever seen this Damon Bailey kid?'

" 'No,' I said, 'I don't believe I have.'

" 'Well,' he said, 'he's a senior in high school and he's going to go play for Coach Knight at Indiana University.'

" 'He must be very good,' I said.

"Several miles passed before he spoke again, and then he said, 'Coach, this kid is the highest scorer in Indiana basketball history.'

" 'Sounds like he's very talented,' I said.

"Another few minutes of silence passed between us, and then he spoke again and said, 'Coach, there is no way we can rightly keep this boy off the All-Time Starting Five.'

" 'Of course not,' I said. 'If the boy is the highest scorer in this state's history, you have no other choice.'

"He nodded at the road ahead of us, but lapsed into silence again. At last he spoke, and said, 'Coach, you know he is a guard.'

"'Is that so? Well, you absolutely have to put him on the team.'

"He turned to me with wide eyes and said, 'Then you won't be upset?'

"And, I looked back at him and said, 'Of course not. Why would I be upset?'

"I let a few seconds pass, and then I said to him, 'But Oscar is really going to be mad.' "

The last time I saw Coach Wooden was in 2001, when the NCAA finals were held at the Metrodome. Clark Kellogg of CBS and I hosted a morning breakfast, at which the coach was presented the NCAA's highest honors. He was frail, but the twinkle was still in his eye, and his love for basketball and the kids who play it was as strong as ever.

Coach Johnny Wooden died at the age of ninety-nine. His records will never be broken. He will be known by those records, and by the people who played for him who, today, credit his coaching—on and off the court—with their personal successes. I will remember him as a gentleman and teacher—a man generous beyond words. And, of course, as the greatest basketball star Lacy Shelby ever saw play the game.

COACH STEBBINS

When you've gone as far as you can, take one more step.

C oach Stebbins was a screamer. He was a banger of lockers and a destroyer of clipboards. He was a firebrand of the first degree, and when he lit into a player or referee, his vocabulary was rich. Many a parent complained to school officials that Coach Stebbins was abusive and harsh. But we all loved him, even those of us who most often felt his wrath.

Coach hated stupid mistakes and lapses in thinking. He fumed when we failed to run plays or see the outlet pass. He bellowed when a ballplayer beat us baseline. Our given names rang off the rafters when we forgot to box out. But the worst thing you could do, in Coach Stebbins's book, was play a basketball game with no heart. He dealt with that crime in the privacy of the cage. Good thing, too. Had the coach ever erupted like that in front of our parents, he would have been arrested for verbal assault with intent to kill.

He could be ugly and he could be personal. He was almost always insulting, and we played better after a dose of his medicine. A typical scene might begin with the players assembled in the locker room at halftime, down by four. The team has sleepwalked through the first two quarters and one or two of the better players have performed below the coach's expectations. While we wait for him to come in, we stare silently at one another. As his footsteps approach, our shoulders tense and we look at the floor. BANG! We flinch in unison as the metal locker door slams against its frame. CRACK! We don't jump this time. We know the sound of a clipboard against the concrete always follows the bang of the locker. Terrible silence.

The coach walks behind us. His breathing sounds like steam escaping from a big engine. Then it begins. Low and controlled at first, then building. "What-in-God's-name-was-that-out-there-tonight?" he'd begin. "Who are you people? Whoever you are, you make me sick to my stomach." Bad basketball always made Coach sick to his stomach, but sometimes it was an individual player who caused him nausea. Then he would say, "Shelby, you make me want to puke."

From there he would take our game apart in the most vivid and exacting language. He humiliated us and made us feel terrible, and we couldn't wait to get back on the court to prove that he was wrong about us. And it usually worked as he intended. The fire he started under us at halftime would fuel a comeback, and after the game he'd rub our sweaty heads and pat our butts and tell us he was proud of the way we played.

But by the time we were seniors, we had grown used to Coach Stebbins's eruptions. The older players who had heard it all so often began to believe the coach only used his anger to motivate. It had become predictable. It was just another gimmick in a coach's bag of tricks. And the wiser we grew, the worse we played.

We managed to struggle our way to the semi-finals of the tournament that senior year. We played terribly the first half and found ourselves down twenty-four when we went to the locker room for halftime. We knew what was coming. The younger players' shoulders tensed up, and when they heard the coach's footsteps, they stared into the floor.

The first thing I noticed was that there was no locker slamming, no clipboard-throwing. The coach came in and paced quietly in front of us, then stopped and said, "I want to apologize to you gentlemen."

We looked up at the coach, then at one another questioningly. "I have failed you," he said softly. "Your talent and hard work got you here, not anything I've done. Oh, I could take credit for one or two victories early in the season, but you've gotten yourself to this game, not me. And now I can't help you. This team you're playing is better than us. They're better coached. And I don't have any tricks left. I honestly don't know what to do."

The coach sat down on the bench and held his head in his hands. We sat motionless as he concluded, "I just wanted to tell you that no matter what happens in the second half, you are the finest group of kids I have ever coached. I am just so sorry that I have nothing more to give you." As he walked out the door, he tapped the assistant coach on the shoulder and said, "You take 'em the rest of the way. I'm going home."

We sat another minute or so before gathering to go back out on the court. Most of us had tears in our eyes. When the second half started, the tears had been replaced by fire. It took fewer than four minutes to erase the twenty-four-point deficit. When the game ended, our second five were on the floor and we were the champs.

For years afterward, I often wondered whether what Coach Stebbins said in that locker room was the anguish of an old warhorse or a slick trick pulled from the bag of a foxy coaching veteran.

But as I've grown older, I've realized that there are no tricks. What Coach Stebbins did was based on an instinct derived from an intimate knowledge of his team. What would work for this team may not have worked for teams past or future. But his accurate judgment of what it would take for *this* team to rise above itself is what made him a genius. I have seen it dozens of times since: basketball coaches purposely getting tossed at a critical moment or a baseball manager thrown from the game with his team trailing. The measure of an act of self-sacrifice is not the outcome of the game, not the score, but whether the members of the team responded by giving more than they thought they had. That night, Coach Stebbins taught us a lesson none of us would ever forget. And it had nothing to do with basketball.

INTO THE REALM
OF POSSIBILITY

When your number is called, it's time to step up.

Life is full of passages. Passages open our world a bit wider to us. Things that had previously seemed impossible, out of reach, fall within our grasp. Our definition of ourselves changes. At the first moment we learn to walk and explore the world around us, we substantially change as people. When we go off by ourselves to our first day of school, the person who returns home in the afternoon is not the one who left that morning. When we solve our first problem without help or stand up for ourselves and our ideas for the first time, we can never go back to who we used to be. We become somebody else with our name and face. We are a step closer to who we will be.

My daughter Ashley, the two-guard on the eighth-grade traveling team, had just completed a passage. It happened in the space of one basketball game. When Ashley woke up the morning of the game, she was a thirteen-year-old girl who loved basketball, hated that she was short, and fantasized of one day being so good that she would become the first woman to play in the NBA. She tempered her fantasy with the reality that her career high game was six points, and that was back in the seventh grade. She knew that if any NBA scouts were nosing around her games, they would probably never notice her. They would probably notice Katie McGlennen.

Katie had been All-World since she was six. She went equally well to her left or right, was a .900 free-throw shooter, was accurate outside as well as in, was the team and the league's leading scorer, and was the only thirteen-year-old girl I knew who consistently faced a box-and-one defense. Suffice it to say that the team, and the coaches, relied on Katie McGlennen. But one weekend, Katie couldn't make it to a tournament game.

"We're going to lose," Ashley said matter-of-factly as we drove to the game. "We always lose when Katie doesn't play."

It was true. But I was one of the coaches of the team, and I couldn't very well tell her she was right, that the situation was hopeless, and that we should all turn around and go home. So I said, "Ashley, you're going to have to pick up the slack. You'll need to go out there and shoot more, get aggressive, take it to 'em," and stuff like that.

"You mean it?" she asked. I had forgotten that eighth graders need permission to shoot. I had forgotten that no one had given her permission before.

The first quarter was slow and ugly. The other team threw up a full-court zone trap, and the better part of the period was spent at their end of the court. The second quarter began with our team trailing by five points and the kids on the bench mumbling something about always losing when Katie wasn't there. But we had installed a press-breaking inbounds play, and to our amazement it worked. Two minutes into the second quarter we were in the lead and Ashley had equaled her career high. And anyone who knew her could tell that Ashley sensed this was her game.

When the horn sounded to end the game, we had beaten the other team 40-25. Ashley had a game high of fifteen, or, as she grew fond of saying, "Five less than half of all the points we scored." She was not the old Ashley, whose previous high game was six. She was now the new Ashley, who has led all scorers, gone five for six from the line, and dropped in two from eighteen feet.

The new Ashley was gentler with her younger sisters. She was now much older than them. She scored fifteen the other day, you know. She was much more patient with her mother, too. The old Ashley had gone the way of bronze baby shoes and photo albums. She was nothing more now than a memory. The new Ashley was here until the next passage, going steady or the NBA, whichever came first.

REMATCH

Prudence is sometimes a scarce commodity.

It was a muggy summer day and hardly anything seemed worth doing. It wasn't just the weather. None of us had felt very enthusiastic about anything for quite a while. Four months back we had been on top of the world. We had managed to take our team through a very rough sectional and on to the semi-state. In order to make it to the finals, we had to beat the top-ranked team in the state. Four of the starting five on their team had already signed letters of intent with Division I schools. But we had managed to win that game by twenty-four points. They had been favored to win by at least that much. Now the press favored us by fifteen over the team we'd face in the finals.

That Saturday night, we had taken the floor confident of victory. The team we had destroyed the day before had beaten this team by twenty during the regular season. They didn't have even one player being courted by a big school. The only thing we knew was that this team had one guy, a point guard, who could shoot. The rest of them, so we were told, were slugs. During the shootaround, we practiced our poses for the next day's sports page.

They scored right off the tip. They kept on scoring. The rumors were wrong. They didn't have only one guy who could shoot; they had twelve. The news also failed to reach us that this team could play defense, too. We just never got started. It was a rout. The referees seemed bored. Our cheerleaders left early. The feeling that nothing much seemed worth doing started exactly when that game ended.

So as the summer heat sweltered and we languished in it, a thought struck Charlie Hixon: "Let's play 'em again."

We turned and looked at Charlie, who had sat straight up with that stupid smile on his face.

"Do what?" I asked.

"Let's play 'em again. And beat 'em this time." Charlie was beaming.

The thought invigorated us like a gust of cold wind. Within minutes, we'd hatched the plan. Charlie would call a cousin of his who lived in enemy territory, and he would pass on the challenge. The state finals teams would meet again, and things would be different. The thought of regaining our pride, setting the record straight, and showing everyone who was number one made us giddy.

Two weeks later, the crowd at the St. Ignatius Catholic Church basketball court was its third-largest in history. The biggest crowd had turned out for the legendary match-up between George McGinnis's pick-up five against Rick Mount and four guys who passed him the ball. The second-largest crowd had turned out when someone thought they saw the image of Saint Teresa of Avila appear on one of the backboards.

The other team showed up without their star shooting guard. Right away we began to think that the drubbing we were about to give these guys would come with an excuse attached, an asterisk: "We didn't have our best guy," they would say. Sure.

The tension hung heavy in the summer evening air. There was no hint of a breeze. The humidity was as high as anyone had ever seen it. Both teams were drenched with sweat after the first minute of lay-ups. This was going to be hard work.

Big Jim Carrie showed up in stripes to officiate. The old man who ran the drugstore on Walnut Street ran the clock for the game. A couple of moms sold Kool-Aid from a big galvanized tub. A shrill blast from Jim Carrie's whistle focused everyone's attention on the center circle.

"Play fair," Big Jim said, and tossed the ball up between the two centers. The other team scored off the tip. On the first possession, I coughed up the ball at half-court, and the guy who replaced their point guard gathered it in and stuffed it so hard that the chain net was still shaking the next time they brought the ball up. Which was sooner than we would have liked. They scored eight points before we got the ball across the ten-second line.

It was just sickening. They destroyed us. Destroyed us on our home court. Destroyed us in front of our families and friends, and destroyed our false pride once and for all.

A small child, the sister of one of our players, came up to us after the game. "Why'd you lose so bad," was the simple, innocent question. The words hung for a second behind my Adam's apple, and then came out like a whisper. "Because they were better than us."

As time went by, the humiliation seemed to pass. We could even laugh about our silly pride and the spectacle we'd made of ourselves, but that was much later. It wouldn't be the last time our pride would get in the way. It wouldn't be the last stupid idea Charlie Hixon ever hatched, not by a long shot. And it wouldn't be the last time we would let our mouths write a check our butts couldn't cash.

I have gotten over just about every aspect of that episode. Except the asterisk. I still can't believe they beat us without their best guy.

CIVIL RIGHTS

Sometimes dreams do come true.

I had not heard of Rosa Parks, the Montgomery bus boycott, the integration of Little Rock Central High School, or freedom rides. In my small world in 1959, the notion of civil rights and discrimination had never crossed my mind. If black people were being oppressed, it wasn't in the gym. Oh, there was talk when, at the end of a sixth grade basketball game, I bear-hugged the other team's guard. He was black, and apparently hugging like that was frowned upon. Neither of us knew that then.

Then one day I was painfully introduced to discrimination, and once I fully understood it, I hated it. I hated it then and I hate it now. I was twelve, and my father asked me what

I wanted to be when I grew up. It was an easy question to answer. I wanted to be a basketball player.

"Who do you want to play for?" he asked.

"The Harlem Globetrotters," I answered without hesitation. Dad chuckled and shook his head. He often did that when I said something stupid. I didn't think my dream was stupid. I loved the Harlem Globetrotters. I knew their history. I knew that once they put their clowning aside, they beat some of the best teams in professional basketball.

My brother, Bob, had taken me to see them play, and Uncle Harry had gotten Bob into the locker room after the night's entertainment. On the back of a Miller High Life label, the guys had signed their names. On that label were the signatures of Tex Harrison, Marcus Haynes, Willie Gardner, and the greatest of them all, Goose Tatum. My brother gave me the label, and I treasured it. Later, when I was in high school, I asked the school band instructor to teach his young musicians to play "Sweet Georgia Brown" as we shot lay-ups before the game. I dreamed of passing the ball around the magic circle and doing tricks with the ball. I had been practicing.

"Why are you laughing at me?" I asked my father.

"Well, you can't play for the Harlem Globetrotters, is why."

"Why not? I could get good enough."

"No doubt," said Dad. "But you can't ever play for them."

"Why not?"

"Because..." he said. "Because you are white."

It made no sense. Black and white ballplayers had always been on the big teams together. Sure, there were some all-black schools, but I just thought that was the way they wanted it.

"You mean they wouldn't let me play, no matter how good I got, just because I'm white?" I asked, incredulous.

"That's right, son," Dad answered. "They wouldn't let you play on their team."

I was thunderstruck. If I had known the words "racial discrimination," I would have used them. But I didn't know such things then. All I knew was that I was sick to my stomach that anyone, regardless of how good he was, could be kept from his dream, simply because of the color of his skin. My young mind began to think of the Globetrotters in a different way.

Time passed. I grew up. I learned the names of Rosa Parks and the Reverend Dr. Martin Luther King, Jr., and my dad walked me through the awful truth about race in our country. I mowed lawns between basketball games in the summer and saved enough to join the Southern Christian Leadership Conference. I watched CBS News and saw students in North Carolina and Tennessee at Woolworth's counters being burned with cigarettes and beaten by white kids who looked like me. I saw grainy black-and-white film of black people in Mississippi trying to register to vote. I saw the fire hoses trained on them, knocking down men and women and children. I saw police dogs biting the leg of a man. The pictures made me sick.

But they also gave me an idea that there was another career path. Maybe I could take pictures like that and tell stories, like the courageous reporters who were being threatened by the mobs of white people. So I didn't become a basketball player. I became a journalist. The guy who tells the story.

Many years later, after I had begun my career in journalism, I found myself drawn to stories of the powerful oppressing the weak, of discrimination and injustice. As the years passed, I won awards, and my father took notice.

"You think you might have a special place in your heart for people who can't live out their dreams in this country because of the color of their skin?" he asked one day.

"I suppose," the boy, now a man, answered his father.

"I mean, you were discriminated against once, weren't you? You sort of knew what it felt like."

"I'm not sure what you're talking about," I replied.

"When your dream of playing for the Harlem Globetrotters was denied," he said, the hint of a smile in his eyes.

I know he was kidding. That tiny moment in the life of an Indiana schoolboy couldn't compare to the horrors of the lunch counter beatings and the taunts and insults during the marches for freedom—the jailings and the lynchings. But perhaps something did happen to me that day I realized I'd never play for the Globetrotters. Perhaps it planted in me empathy and understanding for those who suffer injustice, and a desire to pour light onto those crimes in order that they might be stopped. It's a principle that has guided my career.

Many years later, on a radio show I hosted, I had the immense honor of interviewing Curly Neal, one of the greatest of all of the Harlem Globetrotters. They were in town, and Curly was doing a publicity tour of radio stations. During a commercial break, I told him the story of my childhood dream of playing for the Globetrotters and how it helped shape the rest of my life. He smiled his famous Curly

Neal smile and we finished the interview.

The next day, there were two packages for me at the front desk of the station. One was an authentic Harlem Globetrotters jersey. The other was a framed picture of Curly Neal putting on one of his fabulous dribbling exhibitions. It was inscribed with his signature, and said, "To Don. You should have been a Trotter."

TEACH YOUR
PARENTS WELL

There are times when basketball is not the answer.

I am, and this might be obvious, an extreme basketball
enthusiast. I am also the father of three daughters. You may
deduce from those facts that my children were, you might
say, coaxed into playing basketball. My children might use
other terms to describe my methods of encouragement.
They're grown now, successful women and mothers.

When I think back to when they were kids, I hope
I didn't put too much pressure on them to be basketball
players. I mean, just because basketball is my whole life, they

shouldn't have felt obliged to play. After all, it didn't cost that much to pave the yard and put in the full court with two glass backboards and three-point lines.

The truth is, I encouraged the girls to play basketball, and our family placed a lot of emphasis on practice and discipline and performance. That's why, to me, the story I'm about to tell is all the more remarkable.

The three daughters are Ashley, Lacy, and Delta. Ashley is the oldest and, at fifteen, was the most intense and skilled competitor in the family. Delta, the baby, was twelve, and dreamed of the day when she'd put it in her big sister's face. She had very nice form for a youngster. Lacy, the middle child, was thirteen, and she loved the spirit of the game. But Lacy had been a little slower than her sisters in developing the skills of basketball.

Ashley and Delta made their respective traveling teams that year and Lacy made the B squad. She didn't see much action even at that. She attended all the practices and tried mightily. When she'd boot a pass or get beaten on defense, she'd turn to me with a look of embarrassment. I could sense that she was pained, but she kept on going. I knew that I needed to say something, but I had no idea how to start. Lacy, on the other hand, did.

One night, when I came home from work, Lacy was waiting up for me. Because I worked nights, the house was dark and everyone else was in bed. I was startled when I heard her voice coming from the darkened living room. "Dad, could I talk to you for a minute?"

"Sure," I said, and sat down on the sofa with her. "What's up?"

"Dad," she began, "I have to tell you something that I know will hurt your feelings. I know you will be disappointed in me. But I want you to know that I love you very much and that I'm not doing this to hurt you."

"Doing what?" I asked a little shakily. I had never seen Lacy so serious.

"I have thought about it a long time, Dad," she said. "And I've got to tell you that I don't think I'm ever going to be a very good basketball player. I've tried as hard as I can and I just don't think I'm all that good."

A lump gathered and began to burn in my throat.

"I know how much basketball means to you, Dad," she continued. "I'm sorry if I'm a disappointment to you."

I just stared at my feet, afraid to say anything. The tears welled up in my eyes. You sit there with your heart in your throat, feeling very small about yourself, and wondering where such a child came from. You wonder who taught her to be so gentle and caring. You just sit there.

I finally found enough voice to tell Lacy that I doubted if she could ever disappoint me. I tried to tell her how much I loved her and how proud I was of her, but it must have sounded feeble. I always sound feeble when I have important things to say.

"I like diving," she said, saving me from myself. "I think I could be good at that."

She gave me a hug and ran off to bed. I sat in the dark for a good long while after she left, thinking to myself that there would be no end to the things this kid could be good at.

FOR TOM

"Gone, alas, as our youth, too soon."

The sun beat down on the concrete, the only shadow cast by the backboard bolted to an old telephone pole. It was a humble court, the kind the uninitiated might take for a slab of driveway between the silo and the machine shed where tractors and combines sat quiet and protected. Those who saw only concrete might also miss the fleeting glimpse of Lake Ida visible beyond the hoop. A simple slab of sand and cement, on a farm, by a lake, across the lane from our summer cabin. The place had a name, but I knew it as heaven.

That summer, as I made my way across the lane—basketball under my arm—I was feeling pretty limber. To say I was feeling agile would be stretching the point. The glory years of basketball were nearly thirty behind me. They were also forty years behind Tom, the farmer whose form now cast a new shadow across the court. He was waiting for me, as he had been waiting this time of day each summer. He wasn't only a farmer. One might say that farming was really Tom's hobby. His job, his professional purpose in life, was to coach. Tom was a basketball coach.

It was that fact that had sold me on the cabin two decades earlier. The realtor had said offhandedly, "And if you buy the place, your neighbor will be Tom. He's a basketball coach." I made the deal in the next breath. My wife and children thought I had bought the cabin for the beautiful sunsets across the lake, the solitude, and the promise of good fishing. They were unaware that I had decided on this particular piece of heaven because a basketball coach lived across the lane. I held no one—neither presidents nor kings—in higher esteem. I thought of coaches in the same way I imagined Samurai acolytes beheld the Sensei: possessors of great wisdom, skill, and patience.

We were both too old to duplicate the moves of our glory days, but we could think them. We could imagine them, see them vividly in our minds. Both of us still dreamed heart-pumping dreams of games past. We played each other, one-on-one, rain or shine. I know now that anyone watching us would have seen two old men moving methodically, slowly, even clumsily. No matter. We were the only ones watching, and we saw our former selves. We were fleet of foot and quick as thought itself. We usually played four games to twenty. That was all we had in us most days. The record reveals we split the victories and losses evenly between us.

Tom and I always thought that we would have made a great team, but being fathers of young athletes required us to play against each other. Some evenings his kids would be on my team and mine on his. They were desperate affairs in the heavy heat of summer evenings, but the reward was never the victory. It was the root beer floats waiting for us, post-game, in the air-conditioned kitchen of the farmhouse. There were times when I walked home with the kids after dark and wondered if life could possibly ever be better than this.

One day, a daughter of a friend of ours down the lane stopped by the court and asked if her friends could play basketball on Tom's court. The girl was seventeen; I wondered whether there was a chance for Tom and me to show a couple of kids what basketball was really like. I asked her who her friends were. She said they were just a couple of kids from the college in the town where her sister lived. She said they were basketball players on the college team. I knew the school. I knew it was Division I. I began to think that maybe it was time for Tom and me to go fishing.

The boys showed up at the court to shoot around. We peered from the farmhouse window at a 6'10" behemoth and a 6'5" "guard." A 6'5" player would have been a very tall center on our high school teams, and this ballplayer was the smallest man on his. Tom and I watched through the window as they dunked on the rickety rim. I retreated to the kitchen table, but I noticed Tom was lacing up his Chuck Taylor Converse All-Stars.

"What are you doing?" I asked.

"I think we can take these guys," said Tom. I thought Tom had lost his marbles. I watched as he opened the door and headed to the court. Reluctantly, I slipped into my basketball shoes and followed.

What I witnessed next was something to behold. Tom approached the big boys (Division I) and began running his mouth. I was familiar with his trash talk, but this was from another dimension. It was contagious. I began to talk smack about how good we were and how badly we would spank these young punks. The boys were duly polite and somewhat incredulous that two old guys would actually challenge their (Division I) skills. Smirking, the boys said they'd go easy on us since we were so old.

We shot for first outs. I stepped back off the driveway into the gravel and grass and launched a pro three. *Swish!* The 6'5" point guard missed, and I asked politely whether the shot was outside of his range. Did they have weight training at his school? My eleven-year-old makes that shot consistently, I added. Tom joined in, and by the time we inbounded the ball for the first sequence, the big point guard's confidence had ebbed.

Tom and I were on the same team for the first time. We had paid close attention to each other's game over those years, and we began to play old-fashioned two-on-two basketball. We ran high-low plays, pick-and-rolls, and Tom's block-outs of the big guy cancelled out the boy's ten-inch height advantage. The offensive board was ours, and we kept shooting until we scored.

After three tightly fought games to twenty, the old guys held a two-to-one lead. The smack talk from Tom and me had gotten worse and worse. For a brief moment I began to feel that we were humiliating children and that such behavior from good parents such as the two of us was downright wrong. But it was just a fleeting thought, and the chin music started up again.

I was convinced we had made our point. Two old guys had beaten two young guys who played Division I basketball. It was one of the high points of my life, and I was satisfied and ready for a root beer float. But as I began walking off the court, I heard Tom say to the boys, "Maybe you just aren't used to playing on the confines of a small court. Big-timers like yourselves probably would feel more comfortable and have a better chance of beating us if we were playing, say, full-court basketball inside a gymnasium."

I froze in my tracks. I heard the big guy say that they would kick our butts if only there was a gym around. I cringed as I heard Tom reach into his jeans pocket and produce a ring of keys. Tom was the basketball coach at the high school. It was summer and the gymnasium was empty. Tom had the keys.

The next thing I knew, everyone was piling into cars. All the families up and down the lake lane had heard the news, and they joined the caravan. When we arrived at the high school gym, Tom turned on all the lights and we pulled out the bleachers. The fans took their seats. Tom and I went to one end of the gym and shot around while the Division I players went to their end to warm up.

"Tom," I said under my breath, "This is stupid. I haven't played full-court basketball in twenty years."

"No problem," said Tom. "I'll box this big guy out and you break to the ten-second line on my side. I'll get the outlet to you and then I'll fill the center lane. We'll run them out of the place." He was talking like a coach and I felt good hearing it. It had the effect of deluding me into believing that we could actually do this. Adrenaline, the variety produced by the game of basketball, always made me a little delusional. When we met the boys at half-court for the game to begin, my eyes were spinning like pinwheels and my mouth was speaking the worst kind of smack talk I had ever produced.

Being generous elders, we gave the boys first-outs. Used to five-player team offense, they seemed out of their game. Tom stole the guard's first pass to the big guy; I broke toward our end around the big guard. Tom hoisted a perfect pass over my shoulder for a lay-in. We had the lead.

My heart was beating wildly. The game had been going on for thirty seconds and I needed a substitution. Our defense was part-zone, part man-to-man, part goofy blindness. But the hundreds of games we had played together had given us the gift of second sight. I knew what Tom was going to do and he knew what I was going to do. The big guard kept telegraphing his entry passes, and Tom kept stealing the ball and I kept running the length of the floor, over and over and over again. My face was the color of beet juice and my breathing was coming in audible gasps. Tom had stayed in some kind of shape by running with the teams he coached during the season. He was a man possessed. Not only did he have enough breath to breathe, but he also had enough to continue to talk a blue streak of smack, casting shame and humiliation on these college players.

We continued to run our offense. Tom would post-up and I would cut off his position. He handed off as I ran by, or kept the ball, spun to the basket, and dropped in a lay-up. Sometimes he would get fancy, just to get fancy—and to get the goat of the big guy. Once, on a cut past his post position, Tom kept the ball, but held his position, faked right, and dropped a left-handed behind-the-back bounce pass around the giant. It bounced right into my hands for a reverse lay-up, and the score was 16-10, our favor.

Meanwhile, there was serious talk among the twenty or so spectators that someone ought to call the paramedics. It was that bad. Even Tom began to show the wear of running the length of the full court at full speed over and over again.

Our game began to get sloppy and our legs felt like they were made of Silly Putty.

But Tom's mouth wouldn't stop running. Between gasps, I got in my licks. I had the ball and walked it across the ten-second line. The big guard was playing off of me. I said, "Don't do that. You'd better not do that. You'd better not give me room to shoot this three in your face." I'd been driving off the post for so long that I hadn't taken an outside shot, and he was sinking back to stop the entry pass. I jab-stepped to the right, faked the pass to Tom, and the guard fell further off. I dropped a twenty-two-foot jumper.

"I warned you, dummy," I said. "I warned you I would shoot that three in your face. What's wrong with you? Don't you listen when grown men talk to you?"

The final two came as Tom spun around the big guy and shot a lay-up that one would only see in a game of H.O.R.S.E. We won. The college boys were stunned. They picked up their gear and walked to the door. Most of the fans followed. Before they were out of sight, Tom yelled at the college boys, "Any questions?"

Our families stayed behind. Tom and I waited until the gym doors closed behind the boys and their friends, and then both of us fell to the floor. Tom couldn't feel his fingers. I had charley horses in both thighs that doubled me up into a ball. It took an hour to get the feeling back into Tom's hands and the same amount of time to beat the muscle spasms out of my hamstrings. Our wives and children provided shoulders for us to lean on as we limped to the cars. When we got home, we passed on root beer floats. We took to our beds.

The next morning neither Tom nor I could get out of bed. The pain was indescribable, but it was delicious. In his bedroom in the farmhouse and in my bedroom across the lane in the cabin, Tom and I were thinking the exact same thought: Thank God for basketball. Thank God we won. Someone get me some aspirin, quick.

That great moment in our lives was twenty years ago, now. I think of that game often, but I think of Tom every day. He died of cancer not too long ago. There is a big hole in my heart where he always lived. Now his spirit lives there. With his passing, some things are certain. I will never have a friend like that again in the time I have remaining on this earth. And I will never play basketball like that again. I will never want to. All things must pass. And, with Tom, sometimes that pass was behind the back.

At his funeral, my children brought a wreath for the

ceremony. The kids are grown now and have babies of their own, to whom they will one day tell the story of Grandpa and Tom's game against the college boys. The wreath they chose for Tom and set behind the altar at the church broke my heart when I saw it. It was a beautiful arrangement of flowers, with a ribbon across the front, bearing the simple, deep, and loving single word: Coach.

LESSONS

If life is a game, these are the rules.

Spring arrives. Basketball season ends. Things change and people move on. Coaches move on to other sports, athletes change uniforms, and fans follow their favorites into the next season of excitement.

But there will always be some of us who stay behind, refusing—no, unable—to move on. Some of us will stay behind in lonely, dim gymnasiums for one last shot, just one more hour or two. Some of us will stay forever. That's because we sense somewhere deep inside us that being a basketball player is not just what we do—it is who we are. What we understand of ourselves we learned on the court. Not lessons in hook-steps and lay-ups, but lessons in life.

One of the bestselling books of all time is titled *All I Really Need to Know I Learned in Kindergarten*. The book is sweet and thoughtful, and it suggests the fundamental courtesies taught to us when we were five or six could serve us pretty well as adults. For some of us who spent more time with coaches than teachers and more time with basketballs than books, we learned the most lasting and usable lessons in the gym. The fundamental principles of basketball are, essentially, the principles of a decent life.

LESSON ONE: We play on a team. No matter how great our physical and mental gifts, we cannot inbound the ball to ourselves. We cannot initiate even the simplest play without help. Needing someone is not weakness. It is fundamental to basketball, and to life. Five players with dazzling individual skills who do not play as a team will usually lose. Average ballplayers who share, cooperate, and play to one another's strengths, and who work unselfishly, will discover the magic of a total that is greater than the sum of its parts.

LESSON TWO: The best statistic is an assist. Unselfishness is its own reward. Anyone can shoot. Lots of people can hit. Few have the strength of character to resist the urge to help themselves into the spotlight and instead focus it on someone else. The tallest member of the team is the one who bends to help another.

LESSON THREE: Losing is a part of winning. No one likes to lose and no one should be asked to. But there can be no wins unless somebody posts a loss. Losses tell you something about yourself: primarily, how to improve. Avoiding responsibility for one's role in a loss is self-defeating. Blaming others destroys cooperation and lets us avoid the elemental truth that we all need improvement. Accept responsibility and grow.

LESSON FOUR: Games are won at practice. Anyone who holds back his or her best until the pressure is on will lose. Consistency derives from practice, confidence from preparation, instinct from repetition. In order to be at your best under pressure you must prepare at game speed.

LESSON FIVE: Control the tempo. Knowing when to step up the pressure and when to slow it down is essential in both basketball and life. It is almost always a mistake to increase the tempo of your game when forced into it by the opposition. Answer pressure with calm. Answer panic with level-headedness. Don't be forced to play someone else's game. Play your own with confidence.

LESSON SIX: The best advice sometimes sounds like criticism. No one likes to be singled out for criticism, especially in a crowd. Our reaction is often anger and denial. Usually, it is simply embarrassment. Suffer it and then address the fault. There is little growth until we figure out what we are doing wrong. Sometimes we figure it out for ourselves. More often, someone else has to point it out for us. Either way, use the information to grow.

LESSON SEVEN: Anticipate. Success rests upon your ability to think ahead. Calculating the array of options others may exercise makes you prepared for anything. A person who thinks one, even two, moves or passes ahead will earn many more opportunities than a person to whom everything comes as a surprise.

LESSON EIGHT: Fellowship. We learn that there is more to the game than performance. We allow our hearts to fill with more than pride. We are drawn together by a common idea. We share the extremes of experience and we begin to play interdependent roles in one another's lives. Not everyone will understand and appreciate us. But we will understand and appreciate one another.

LESSON NINE: Time-out. There are times in life and in basketball to stop. No points are given for continuing past the point of exhaustion or effectiveness. Time-outs are no admission of failure. Use them effectively to rest and to analyze your next moves. The smartest time-outs are those called just before it becomes obvious to everyone else that one is needed.

LESSON TEN: Love. You can't simply like what you are doing and do it to its fullest. You cannot demand of yourself dedication unless you love the object of your dedication. You cannot love something until you have come to respect and appreciate its detail, and until you have sacrificed a part of yourself for it.

Some of us have learned these lessons and some of us still think of ourselves primarily as basketball players. We may have chosen for ourselves the role of a banker, a cook, a lawyer, a plumber, or a journalist, but we wake up mornings and look in the mirror and see a basketball player. We play our lives by the rules of the game, and every day we employ the lessons we learned on the court.

As the gyms empty out, some of us will stay behind. Sure, we'll fish, knock out some fly balls, ride bikes, throw a few spirals, swim, or run a mile or two, but for us, the season never ends. Not until we have dribbled off this mortal coil. No, for us there is only one season. Some people call it basketball. We call it life.

ACKNOWLEDGMENTS

I would like to thank, first, my daughter Ashley Shelby, of Mill City Writers' Workshop: basketball player, mother, author, and editor, who believed these stories should be made into a book. She edited every word of the manuscript, dealt with the publisher, and handled this matter as finely as she ran the point as a player.

I want to thank all the coaches of youngsters. You work for little glory, you have sacrificed much, you are committed to the kids and the game. Good coaches, who teach the bigger lessons, are, and always will be, my heroes.

I thank Coach Tubby Smith at the University of Minnesota and his wife, Donna, for allowing me into their lives, and for all the good they've brought to the game and the players lucky enough to have known them.

To Chris May, Executive Director of the Indiana High School Basketball Hall of Fame, for his guidance.

To Kevin Mulder, who came up with the most distinctive name for a basketball newspaper, the *Full-Court Press*. That newspaper published many of these stories under his editorship, and later under the direction of Keith Wandrei, to whom I owe a deep debt of gratitude.

To Ken Lien, who asked me to host the Mr. and Ms. Basketball award banquet for more than twenty years. Thank you for your love of the game, the players, and for your faith in me.

I want to thank all of my teammates over the years for the great fun and terrible seriousness of our time on the court together.

And finally, to my wife and daughters Delta and Lacy, for sharing me with that other love, basketball.

ABOUT THE AUTHOR

D on Shelby is widely considered one of the best, and most decorated, local news anchors and reporters in the country. He has won three National Emmys and two George Foster Peabody awards, which are the broadcast equivalent of the Pulitzer Prize. He was awarded the National Distinguished Service Award by the Society of Professional Journalists, the International Radio and Television News Directors Association's First Place honors for International Investigative Reporting, and Columbia University's duPont Award for Investigative Journalism. He retired from daily reporting and anchoring in November 2010, after forty-five years in the industry.

Shelby was also a basketball player, leading his team to the 1965 Delaware County (Indiana) championship, scoring twenty-five points in the final game, and being named to the All-County All-Star Team. He was inducted into the Delaware County Sports Hall of Fame in 2003.

As an adult, he coached his daughters' teams for seven years, while continuing to pound the hardwood himself. He played on a 35-and-over men's team that won the Minnesota State Amateur Basketball Championship title seven times.

Despite his professional accomplishments in the field of broadcast journalism, the face he shaves every morning is still that of a seventeen-year-old basketball player.